A Busine
Journey
For Tigers

By Angela Fumpson

ISBN: 978-1-9993688-0-7

Email: info@white-tiger.co.uk

Cover, layout and artwork by Mark Guatieri - Brand51
Photography donated by Rupert Dean - Colibree Tours
Print edition printed and bound in Great Britain by Doveton Press Ltd.

This book was printed using paper from sustainable wood sources

Foreword

Systems, systems, systems, yawn, yawn, yawn......when Angela first asked me to read her book and invite me to write a forward about it, my heart went in my mouth and I was trying to work out how to tell her that I couldn't or wouldn't write a foreward on a book about such a subject. I'm a touchy feely sort of bloke and very quickly switch off when there is a need for attention to detail and naturally gravitate towards the human element of life. Having worked with hundreds of business owners over the last decade, I've seen many gravitate towards the task and many others gravitate towards the people side of business and even more struggle to straddle that divide between the two. This book does that.

I can remember meeting Angela for the first time about four years ago and was fascinated by this person who was a ball of nervous energy, with lofty spiritual ideals and a down to earth and pragmatic approach to systemising business. She didn't make sense to me at first and then when I started to appreciate her motivations which predominantly revolve around her family and white tigers, I realised where the drive was coming from. I know that her writing this book will have taken her well and truly out of the proverbial comfort zone and it's been a pleasure to see her get down on paper her ideals which embrace this elusive combination between the 'hard' and 'soft' of business.

As a Non-Executive Director for a small number of businesses and having come from a background of business ownership, management and business coaching, I see the most successful of businesses be driven by an utmost respect for their customers and a drive towards creating a win:win relationship with all concerned. They have a drive towards delivering a level of customer experience that is not only market leading and of value to the customer but is consistent. Inconsistently good customer experience is worse than delivering a consistently average experience. As consumers, we are more demanding than we ever have been and the paradox is that many a demanding business owner moans and whinges about the poor experiences they have received as customers and at the same time head businesses that are bringing a less than good experience to their own customers. This book, and more importantly working through the exercises in this book, brings consistency to performance.

The successful businesses all have a clear purpose. Often it's an individual drive to achieve something that validates them and others have a more altruistic drive towards doing something that brings value to many. One is arguably better than the other, but either way, those business owners driven by such a deep rooted need all understand the relationship between ideal and delivery. Angela's exercises throughout the book take those of us who haven't naturally embraced this relationship through a practical and challenging journey that helps us bridge that gap. The fact that you are reading this book suggests that you might be the type of person who seeks to learn from others. In my coaching travels I have met many a person who was an avid reader and who did nothing with the learnings and I've met many more people who already know everything that there is to know and who will not get upset with that statement as they won't be reading this book anyway. Ignorance is one thing but wisdom without application is on another level all together, so if you are serious about getting the most from this book then do the exercises and then put the resultant findings into practice in your business. Otherwise, I would suggest you don't waste your time.

Enjoy your journey of discovery and embrace those elements of Angela's book that you find most challenging, as they are the areas that you need most of all to be working on. And above all, have fun putting the book into practice because if you do, you will find that you and those around you will have more fun thereafter as a result.

Rob Carter
Non Executive Director and Business Coach

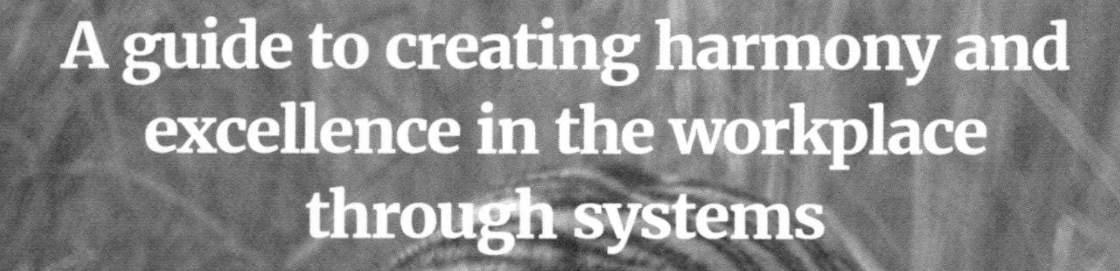

A guide to creating harmony and excellence in the workplace through systems

"Be the change you want to see in the world"

Mahatma Gandhi

With many thanks to Rupert Dean of Colibree Tours for the donated Tiger images

Introduction

Why did I write this guide? Well I have many reasons but I will share the three closest to my heart.

1. I wanted a product for the Tigers -
My passion other than my family is preserving the Tigers. This beautiful creature has been a love of mine since knee high and in particular the White Tiger. I was brought up in Wales but had family in Portishead so spent many days coming over the Severn bridge and loved to spend time gazing at the White Tigers in Bristol Zoo. I was obsessed by the wonderful creatures and grew up with pictures, posters and anything with big cats on it. I have always been drawn to and worn Tiger's eye semi-precious stone; I know now what I am destined to do.

2. As a business mentor, good listener and shoulder to cry on I see a lot of the same problems occurring from business owners. When we get stuck, for whatever reason, it is possible to forget the passion that drove you to start it all in the first place. If problems go unchecked they can not only impact your business but your personal life and your team. I have become that thought partner for many; being part of the conversations that previously they would have only had with themselves. Airing the business worries that keep you awake at night, getting them out of your head and a new perspective on what you can do about them is invaluable. For me too I believe everybody needs a mentor and accountability buddy. My skill is being able to step back and think logically about the how, focusing on the every detail that turns the dream into a deliverable. I don't want to make everyone love systems but realise the important part they play and to think about making an investment in them just as they would their sales or marketing.

3. This book is also part of my own self-development - my advice, never stop investing in yourself whatever form that needs to take. Sharing my knowledge, seeing my thoughts and experience in print and more important to me seeing others benefit and feedback was really important to my growth. I have been in engineering for over twenty years developing products and solutions; now I am out there sharing my knowledge and my way of doing things. Writing is my way of improving my own confidence and to realise my dream in White Tiger..

By you purchasing this book today you have contributed money to saving the Tigers from extinction so well done and a big thank you goes out from me.

Who is the book for

This book is for anyone serious about improving the way their business operates and who want consistency and predictability in the way they deliver to their customers. Striving for excellence in what they do. If you recognise any of the symptoms below then I am confident this book will help you find your next steps. You must be ready to step up and accept change, this book is a workbook and demands action if you want to see results.

- Fire fighting,
- Searching for information,
- Too many spreadsheets
- Experiencing rapid growth,
- Searching for information,
- Confusion not clarity,
- Too many meetings,
- Customer complaints,
- No time or headspace.

What will you gain from reading this book

My message is simple - Clarity and harmony in the workplace and that is what I want for you. To be able to see where you are, how your systems have evolved and what you need to do next. To be able to streamline your business process and take the guesswork out of running the business.

You will:

- Understand what a business process and system is.
- Assess your own system.
- Know what factors stop your business system working effectively.
- Learn a visual way to step back and look at your business.
- Have a tool for prioritising improvement action.
- Learn some strategies to make change stick.

If even one person comes back and says I can finally take that holiday that was forever in the planning phase. Then I'm happy. Your system should help you to step back out of the business and facilitate the growth journey.

My thanks

I have to take a moment to thank my family, friends and my colleagues (you know who you are as there a too many to mention) without your support, help and hardwork White Tiger would never have been realised. It is the people around me that have shared the vision and believed in me and my ways that feed my strength and energy to push forward.

This book is dedicated to Dad who walks with me in spirit.

Setting the scene

This is a journey, a journey into your business system. To introduce you to a new way of thinking or perspective that can identify positive change to support your business growth. This isn't a heavy technical or reference book, more a workbook and thought process for the journey.

The way to use this book is to follow chapter by chapter so that like a system you stay on the path of the journey with me. This is my perspective: some will love it others may disagree but it's out there. I will teach you the basics, the need to know stuff and the important points to pay attention to. Your job is the "I get it now" or "light bulb moment" on how you can apply my thoughts to your business and transform it ready for your future growth.

How to use this book

As you work through this book I will be asking you to carry out some exercises, it is part of the thought process on the journey. Many of my 1 to 1 sessions start to produce life changing thoughts and copious note writing, and lightbulb moments! That is what I want for you.

There are designated areas in the book for you to write notes, I advise you to take time out to think and record your thoughts - these points will be relevant as you move through the book and you will refer back to them. One way of tackling this is to set yourself weekly challenges, maybe a chapter a week so that you can then observe the following week with new thought and mindfulness. Use the light bulb boxes they will be too precious not to capture.

Lastly remember to put into action what you find, don't be the person that reads much without that knowledge actually impacting your decision making. Feel free to share the knowledge and help many but remember each workbook someone uses raises money for a good cause.

Your journey through this book

Chapter	Your personal Journey	Business clarity	Chapter wins
Chapter 1: (Pg 9) How did you get here?	Revisit your journey so far, emotionally connect. Set out your intentions - what do you want from this book?	The story behind the business and its growth. Assess the business system status quo. Where has the 'norm' come from and who holds the power to change.	Reconnect with the business, build your business story for communications. Gain a starting point and what you want to change.
Chapter 2: (Pg 19) We have procedures - why do we still get problems?	**Culture & People** Impact and understanding	Understand why things happen and what our business climate is. Look at triggers and resistance.	How will this process benefit others and how do you motivate for change. Start to plan your approach to improvement.
	Systems Understand what a system is and what you have	Observe how you work currently and what affects your ability to deliver your goals.	What to consider when writing a system and how you know it is effective. Plan how your systems will be written.
	Control & Reliability How to enable others to make better decisions freeing you up from the control	Setting boundaries for decision making through values and vision.	What information does your team need? Defining information and KPI's for your system.

Chapter	Your personal Journey	Business clarity	Chapter wins
Chapter 2: We have procedures - why do we still get problems?	**The Approach** Increase your awareness of how others feel, understand if your perception is correct. **Resources** How do you hear about issues? Are there any barriers to open communication? Harnessing the power of your team, small steps can lead to big change.	How well does your team understand the part they play in the vision? How involved do they feel? Understanding day to day issues. Preparing for ideas flow and supporting the process.	Understand the barriers to change and your team - prepare for your approach to change Planning to support change, understanding how problems are currently communicated.
Chapter 3: (Pg 54) Learnings	Personal journey check-in, noticing and learning to process emotion and understanding the feelings that are being generated on the journey.	Summarising what has been looked at so far in terms of People and Process.	Stopping, pausing and taking a moment to see where you are on the journey, preventing information overload.

Your journey through this book

Chapter	Your personal Journey	Business clarity	Chapter wins
Chapter 4: (Pg 57) Looking at the big picture	Learning about the process map and how and who should walk your customer journey	Taking the initial snapshot and review of the business process	Learning more about your front line team roles and identifying your champions for change.
Chapter 5: (Pg 69) Gathering your thoughts	Stopping overwhelm, maintain motivation; the importance of looking after you and celebrating your achievements.	Draw your process map	Harnessing improvement ideas, seeing the big picture
Chapter 6: (Pg 77) So what now, using your process flow mapping to drive change?	Preparing for change, learning to share and create the buzz for your vision. Understanding how the information collected affects change and being mindful of the relevant pain points that affect change.	Prioritisation and planning for change.	Understanding the sequence - Vision, strategy, planning, testing, action, celebration

Chapter	Your personal Journey	Business clarity	Chapter wins
Chapter 7: (Pg 83) Recap	Understanding the journey steps	Checklist for the business journey	Gap analysis and understanding where more detail and research is required.
Conclusion (Pg 85)	You have the power to change	The way forward	Inspiration
Appendix A (Pg 86)	Information on ISO9001	Understanding the benefits of ISO9001	Quick guide to ISO9001
Appendix B (Pg 87)	Information on Ishikawa Diagram	More structured brainstorming	How to organise ideas and solutions
Appendix C (Pg 89)	Information on flowcharts	Understanding symbols and use, including crafting your own symbolisation	Quick guide to flowchart symbols
Appendix D (Pg 90)	Information on Tiger process for prioritisation	Improving prioritisation methods	Given template for prioritisation

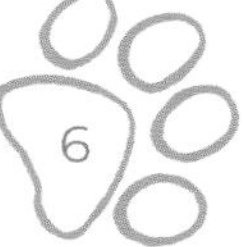

The Basics - the techie bit!

What do we mean by a system?

For everything we do, we have a way of doing it - a process.

A process as defined in the dictionary is - " A systematic series of actions directed to some end or a continuous action, operation, or series of changes taking place in a definite manner".

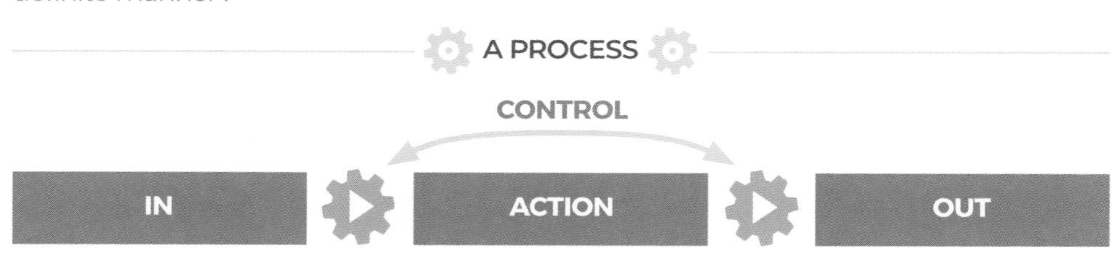

We take inputs in the form of materials or information and we carry out an action on them. We then get a different result or product that we will pass on to the next stage or to the customer. As shown by the diagram we also have controls in place to ensure that the process that we have designed actually takes place.

What we do then is have countermeasures in place, therefore if the desired outcome or output is not as we want it there is another path to go down.

This may sound a bit of a mouthful but it is basically getting, doing, results & control!

Lots of these processes together make your system, for example your sales process, your costing or quoting, your scheduling, your operations and your accounts. They all have a process for doing things and together they make up your business system.

These processes interact with one another and work in harmony to achieve your objectives and in turn deliver your purpose and vision. Quite often it is the human interactions between these processes that needs addressing, it is the interrelation between the processes that can mean all the difference to a company's performance. We have all heard the phrase 'it's not my job', or have experienced the over the wall to the next department scenario. Harmony is about changing the culture and removing blame, when we look to the system for the problem things change. Maybe it was nobody's job, just maybe there is a gap in the process that was missed. Each and every person should be looking out for each other as a team, a company is a living organism and these people to people relationships and links are key.

Imagine a world where your staff are saying to each other "how can I make your day today?" or "What do I need to do in my job that will give the next person in line the right things to make them succeed at their job." When you study your business processes with these questions in mind; you end up with a company that runs like a well oiled machine.

My first goal is to get you clearly thinking about the business objectives that reflect your purpose. When you have clarity you can set about designing a planned, efficient and effective way of meeting these objectives. With one important thing in mind - the people, engage your team from the start.

We need to think about changing our ways for the better, only then will we see the culture and the results we want and expect.

> **Henry Ford said:**
> "If you always do what you've always done, you'll always get what you've always got."

Redesigning and restructuring in companies is something that has been spoken about for many years, but we have to be careful that we fully understand the needs behind our actions. We want things to be predictable and repeatable but we need to build flexibility into our systems so that they can grow with us. We sometimes design processes around software packages or set solutions but we need to design for purpose & implementability. Dr Deming was very clear about this when he said "If you can't describe what you are doing as a process, then you don't know what you are doing" Strong words but I believe with guidance everyone can learn to look at what makes their customer journey such a success and explain it as a business process.

The first thing on any company's agenda after answering the question "Why do we exist" in my eyes is to identify the day to day company decisions and processes to achieve that purpose. Your roles and processes need to be as simple and logical (to the user) as possible. When you have designed what you want on paper or maps then, and only then, do you automate it.

I would love to be able to give you the magic blueprint for a business process that gives the right answer to a problem every single time. The truth is it depends on how you work, your industry, the company's life cycle, the competition, the culture and countries you operate in and lots more factors - there is no one magic formula. Every company may have similar key activities but how you do them makes you who you are.

When you are starting with a clean slate and fantastic idea this is a lot easier, but when you have established cultures and ways of doing things you need a different approach. I think it is important at this stage to look at how your company has evolved.

Chapter 1:

How did you get here?

For most companies that I talk to there has been a great idea that then becomes a feasible business opportunity. The story and purpose evolve and the company starts to grow as demand increases. For some this can happen very quickly and get out of control, unfortunately for some this has caused the demise of the company.

One quote sticks in my head from a very promising company called Dijwans. This was a company that had a good product related to mapping networks of web content but it epically failed as a start up missing the detail. I cannot find the reference now but I remember it was a quote from an article in Forbes from the Dijwans leaders;

> "A good product idea and a strong technical team are not a guarantee of a sustainable business. One should not ignore the business process and issues of a company because it is not their job. It can eventually deprive them from any future in that company".

Successful companies don't ignore anything, they innovate and when it works they systemise it. Systems don't have to restrict, they don't cause these companies to stand still; they just help make every improvement a habit. An effective system supports the vision & goals of your business and enables you to lead from a position of authority, making good fact based decisions. Taking the guesswork and assumption making out of running the business. In turn, this fosters the right culture, and with good leadership you can inspire people to achieve more than they ever thought possible.

What I want you to do is take a moment to think how it all started. If you were not the person that created the business talk to others; find out the story behind the company how did the structure build up? Think in terms of changes in the organisational chart; how did the company build in numbers? I am not about to tell you the right way I just want you to record the important points to go back to. In a moment I will be asking you to carry out your first exercises and you can use the pages in this book to record your thoughts, plans and capture light bulb moments along the way. In fact as we work through the book we will be referring back to these points for further discussion. Just before you go and research your company story let's look at why we need to do this.

The business journey

The reason I asked you to think specifically about how you grew in numbers and recruited is because this is often how procedures start. Imagine for a moment company xyz, they are a partnership and have one member of staff, June in the office. Suddenly they start to find larger and more demanding projects; another consultant joins them; they need somebody to manage sales or perhaps administration of projects. In steps George just at the right time, a keen individual and eager to learn. If fact they decide he will be a great asset to the company and bring him in on a trial basis to start helping June. On his first day June explains what goes on in the office and George writes it down so that he won't forget. George is so good at writing everything down that they decide to use his notes as their first procedure, and so the system starts to be born. Next they need to make sure that the new consultant takes all the details they need and key points so they create a checklist, does this sound familiar? The story could go on but I think you get the picture.

I am not saying that getting organised like this and writing everything down is wrong, but I have rules around creating procedures and looking at the big picture. These I will share with you later in the book but for now can you see that the procedures for company xyz had been written by the most inexperienced person in the company? Do you think that this is right?

This may or may not be similar to your story, I know many owners that have thought very hard about their systems. They have spent many hours writing procedures for each part of the business, sometimes I see large manuals full of operational procedures. One business I know detailed how reception should open up and select tunes on Spotify, the trouble is procedures written this way can be pages and pages long and do not get read; they are also not easy to dip in and out of if you forget something. Staff need to be given responsibility and decision making in order for them to grow, therefore it is all about balance, identifying risk and applying control through writing a procedure. Please bear in mind that everyone also learns and takes in information differently, with new technology there is so many creative ways to get a message across.

Your journey

As with everything there is an inner and outer journey, for me it is about putting the people and the processes together to work in harmony. We have looked at how your business structure came into existence but what about your personal story? How did you get to where you are today?

If the business is your creation then write about why you started, fall in love with that reason all over again, feel the excitement! I want you to reconnect again so that you are excited about designing the ultimate dream business, it's ok not to get excited about systems but emotionally connecting with the result will drive your action tenfold.

If you are not the owner then why did you join, take time to learn the story behind the business purpose. What do you want to achieve from this journey, both for you and the business? It may take a while to answer some of these questions so be patient and spend time on them. Your business or role in the business is there to support the life you want to lead - it is a vehicle, an enabler. It is not there to just provide financial reward, please remember not everything is about the destination the fun and growth happens on the journey! If your values are not in line with the company values and ethos how can you take pleasure from what it does? Conflict will cause stress and disrupt the harmony needed for a smooth decision making process. This is such an important point to get to grips with, I want everyone to love what they do; do you?

Let me introduce you to your first light bulb moment! Use these thought bubbles every time you get new thought or light bulb moment or even note something that you want to devote more time to.

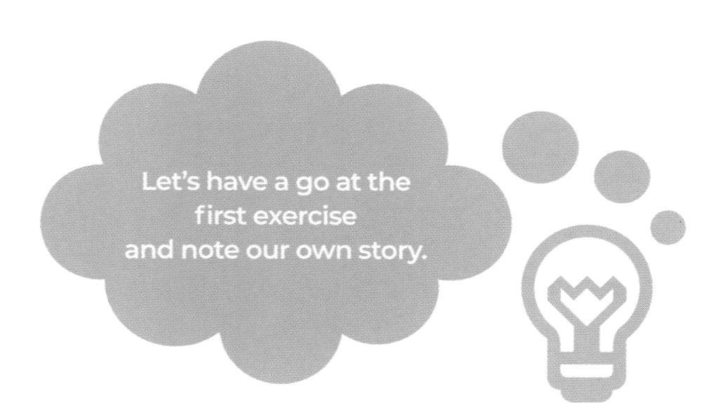

Exercise Time

I would like you to take a moment to think about what we have discussed so far and carry out the following exercises. The first is about how you and the business have evolved and the second is to note in what form you communicate your story & procedures / system to your team. Take your time over them before moving on.

Exercise 1 - The story behind the business?

Firstly I would like you to think about how and why the company was created, record the story here.

Exercise 2- Your own journey?

What is your story, how did you get where you are today? Try to link emotionally with the reason for starting or joining the company, is that connection still present today or has it changed?

Exercise 3 - How did the company system grow?

At what stage of the company's life were your procedures written (if you have them)? Are they still the same today or are they regularly reviewed and updated? Think about how a process becomes the norm, where none exist who holds the key to the knowledge?

Exercise 4 - What are your aims for this journey?

What do you want to get personally out of the journey? Think not just about better systems for the business but what in turn that means for you personally, whether it is more time, headspace or even an exit strategy.

The system

We have researched about our own journey the business creation story, looking at how our processes and systems came about but what format are they in? Do you have paper manuals, a server, all in the cloud or interactive video? There are so many innovative ways of sharing information today that I think it is important to note where you hold the information. I believe all companies should be learning organisations with a hub of knowledge that is accessible to those when they need it on their own learning pathway through the company. Understanding how this information is best presented and where is very important; as is when it is required.

Exercise 5 - How do you communicate the purpose & process?

How do you communicate your story to staff? Do they know your intentions, vision or purpose? Do they understand why they do what they do and how they fit in to the big picture?

Exercise 6 - What format is your system in?

1. If you have systems in place in what format are they (written word, diagrams, checklists, video, flowcharts etc..). Who has access to your procedures?

2. If there are changes how do you cope, is there someone responsible for this?

As you work through the exercises in this book I feel sure you will begin to see my thinking and reasoning behind the questions. Don't worry if they feel awkward or strange at first this is an awakening process too a personal journey shall we say. You may or may not be getting many thoughts on paper but either way it's ok, you could get ideas at any time so carry around the book and use the lightbulb moments. It will be a way of organising your thoughts in relation to the journey you are on.

I will also be asking you to observe things during your week at work, focusing on specific elements as issues arise. You can also use the lightbulb spaces for writing observations. It is amazing what you notice when you look with a different perspective & systems thinking!

A final word on your journey

What do I want? You to design, innovate and make things the norm, engrain it as part of your grand system. Make it fit your business and people, get everyone involved and contributing to your success.

In this chapter you have thought about how everything started and how your business has grown; including what processes you have in place. With this you should now have assessed who created the processes, what format are they in and how you communicate them.

You should now have spent time on thinking about you and your personal journey, taking time to reflect on what you want from the journey.

Lastly how do you update things when they change, this final question was to start to look at responsibilities for your process control. Something that goes hand in hand here is how you know changed information has been received, read and understood. You may also start to see any power houses in the organisation as I like to call them, those who hold knowledge and become a go to person and hence enjoy the power that brings.

We need to take responsibility for how we communicate what we want from our people & business. When things aren't going right you can only blame yourself because the results you get are directly related to the quality of information and instruction you give out. Of course people will only follow and value the system if they see you using it and not taking shortcuts! If we want to lead by example we need a system that we can follow so easily it is second nature, that is why it needs to be designed to fit your business and way of working. If people do not follow the system it is usually because they have either not been shown, found a better way, the system is not logical / hard to follow and they do not buy into it.

My first task for you regarding observations is probably the biggest of the fact finding exercises, I want you to know how things work at the front line. Don't worry if this takes time, make time for those important conversations and just watch and listen. Be mindful of the answers you have for the first exercises and any differences you observe first hand.

Things to observe over the next week:

- What are people using in your business to tell them how things are done?
- Where do they get their information from?
- Observe whether people are travelling and searching for information during the day.
- Take time to ask people if they find what exists useful, do they know a procedure exists?
- Ask someone what they would find useful in their job or as a training aid.
- Most important is how would they like to receive the information required to do their job well?

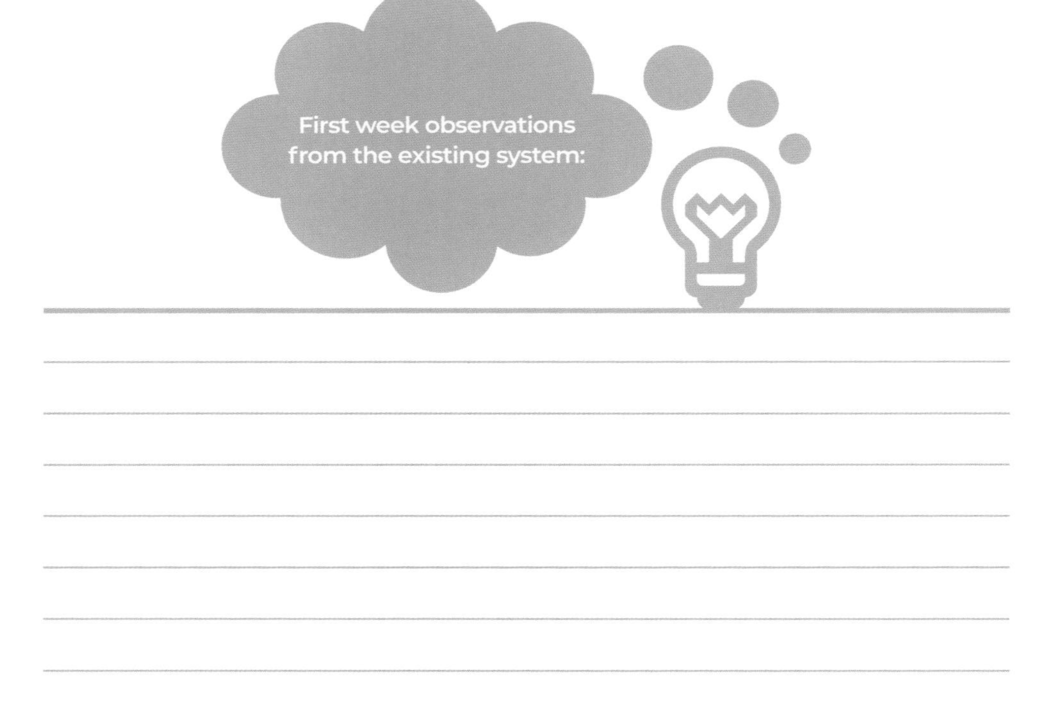

Chapter 2:

We have procedures - why do we still get problems?

'We have been there, done that, written it all down - and they still don't do what we ask! All it has done is just created more paperwork; it just benefits the auditor and everyone hates having to do it.'

How many times have you heard a conversation like this? Why do you think processes fall down?

I am not claiming that systems are the only magic formula but with the right approach they add value and structure for your success. Conversations like the one above particularly happen when I am discussing the implementation of standards such as ISO9001 (refer to appendix A for information). Guides and standards such as ISO9001 are proven templates that have been used for years and evidence has been shown multiple times by the International Standards Organisation surveys that the result is improved performance, quality and sales.

I believe the secret to these success stories is using the correct approach, understanding and application of the standard. This is also a passion of mine - educating companies on the correct interpretation and use of the ISO9001 standard. The motivation behind why they want the certificate usually is an indicator to the success of the system (and usually determines whether they are a good fit for working with me or not).

If we think about the journey of systemising your business this discussion becomes even more relevant because the motivation for the changes and internalisation of the system have a major effect on its success. Make sure you complete the initial exercise on this, in fact let's make this the next exercise; write down why you are on this journey, what made you pick up my book and persevere with reading it (especially if you are like many and hate the detail stuff)!

Now what about your people, what impact is this journey going to have on them? If you are going to motivate them in this change then you need to be able to answer the question "what's in it for me?"

Take 5 minutes now to reflect and note down the answers to these questions. If it helps put it up on the wall to stay motivated and tell others.

Name your top 3 reasons for wanting to work on your business process / system.

1

2

3

What is your ideal outcome and result of putting in or improving your business process? Put your vision in the light bulb, imagine you are writing a press release or company blog.

Name the top 3 reasons that your staff will benefit in this exercise and change process.

1

2

3

So let's pause here and go back to our thought journey and reflect; we have our beginnings, our vision and are committed to the journey. So why with all these good intentions do projects fail? We will break it down and look at the issues that may have caused discussions like the one at the start of this chapter to occur. All of the following topics listed overleaf, can have an impact on how your system & hence business functions, each one if ignored could impact the success of the business. Issues can be internal or external factors but for the purpose of this book we are concentrating on the internal factors that we have a degree of control over.

As we go through this chapter it will be useful if you can relate discussions to your own situation. Keep in mind your answers from chapter 1 and how the creation of your system has impacted on these areas. This is not an exhaustive list but common issues I have experienced, the areas we will cover here are:-

- People & Culture
- The Method and format of the system.
- Control, checks and reliability of the system.
- The approach taken when created.
- The resources - machines, equipment, technology and infrastructure.
- Conflict & Change

Some of you may recognise that these together become very similar to the Ishikawa or fish bone diagram, used to determine cause and effect. If you are not familiar don't worry but I can highly recommend its use to structure your brainstorming as you find solutions to everyday problems. The diagram gives structure and organisation to the thought process, I have included more information just as an aside for research later within Appendix B.

Let's take a look at the above issues in depth so that we can gain a deeper understanding of how problems evolve and how they relate to the success of a system.

People & Culture

What do I mean by culture? We will all have a different understanding in our minds by what is meant by organisational culture. We may find it difficult to define precisely as it may be more of a feeling to us. People are often not consciously aware of it, but it can have a major influence over how individuals behave and react to situation and changes. A common way to think about culture is 'the way things are done around here'. There will be an underlying acceptance about what is acceptable and not acceptable behaviour in the company, a collection of values whether company enforced or created by the workforce. Quite often it's the informal organisation that exists behind or under the face of the company.

I am especially interested in creating clarity and harmony where there is only one culture in the workplace; no hidden agendas. I want you to think about your culture as the climate for the business, just like our weather report. It is made up of many factors that combine to give us the effects we see. I would define it as made up of your hierarchy, relationships, interactions in terms of your processes, objectives, how you treat your team, different personalities and the leadership style that exists.

Add to this the pressures of major company events and history like mergers or staff movement and individual/personal issues and emotional baggage carried and you see the complexity that grows. Your own climate will have an influence on the level of morale and attitudes which your team exhibit at work. It will affect their relationships and their performance/productivity. It will also have a big impact on the way individuals react to particular situations that arise, like a change to the system.

There are many ways that you can assess your company climate and factors that are currently influencing the climate. I personally like to start off with the good old fashioned 'management by walking around' theme. One way I help to gain a perspective on company climate with my clients is to carry out an independent and anonymous assessment. I interview a good cross section of staff and I include all keys figureheads. As an independent person with no company history or politics, just there to help and improve. I get some overwhelming responses just by providing a vent for their frustrations. In most cases the candidates are so grateful to unload their concerns and feelings that I really get an insider view of the company, of course I take these confidentially. I also ask them about their aspirations and personal goals. I collate all the results and tactfully feedback to the business owners. Most owners are very grateful of knowing the underlying issues, gaining a perspective that they otherwise would not have found. Sometimes in our day to day role it can be difficult to put ourselves into a position where we understand another perspective, especially if we have never worked in that area or job. It is also hard for some individuals to speak up against another manager or superior in a hierarchical climate. Think about how you can open up conversations within your company, as I talk about later in this book it may be that you do not do this personally but choose another person to do it.

Often it may be the small things that happen that have added up over time, stirring often strong emotion or resentment in employees that has never been voiced due to the culture. Finding and solving these true root issues will help stop the negative culture from undermining all the good intent. It all comes back to relationships, honesty and sharing for me, I love this quote it says family to me yet this is a huge company.

"The only thing we have is one another. The only competitive advantage we have is the culture and values of the company. Anyone can open up a coffee store. We have no technology, we have no patent. All we have is the relationship around the values of the company and what we bring to the customer every day. And we all have to own it." **Howard Schultz, CEO, Starbucks**

How many of you have walked into Starbucks to find someone genuinely asking about your day and caring? How special did you feel? Yes there is a system behind it / a process but the way you treat your team will come out in how they treat your customers and often each other.

We have to lead by example, I know it is possible to change and cultivate the right climate and change a negative one. All it takes is one good leader and the tribe will form and influence the rest; then we create leaders at every level of the business.

My experience over the years had led me to the conclusion that companies that have been designed well with exceptional leadership throughout all levels achieve outstanding results. The winning mindset creates winning companies, where they may fall down is when they become overburdened and do not have the right backup to take it to the next level. We need to learn to embrace the team, creating, training and supporting our leaders. We find if we do not prepare our structure for growth there is a lack of process to support the increase in staff numbers, sometimes we outgrow our systems because they have not been designed or planned with the growth and intention in mind. If processes have been developed piecemeal (more on this later) then this is a sure sign of hitting this bursting point. On occasion I find that an old embedded process is reinforcing a bad practice or negative culture instead of creating good, this needs to be identified and nipped in the bud early. If your system is designed to grow as the company grows and you continue to monitor its effectiveness you should be continuously improving and developing - this is where I want you to be. The learning organisation.

As the next exercise I want you to think about your culture carefully, be honest about your leadership styles. Think about your personality type and the dynamics of your team, there are too many products on the market to discuss personality profiling here but it may be something that you would like to read up on. I read every day for personal development - something I would highly recommend. Basically most profiling tools look at key personality characteristics whether they classify them as a colour, animal or behaviour, what they set out to do is understand the behaviour traits of individuals. If we understand why we behave the way we do; what our strengths and weaknesses are; then we can start to understand the dynamics of our team and work together better. Just be careful not to start pigeon-holing people into their personality boxes.

Let's use Disc as an example, the letters stand for:

- Dominance - Your typical entrepreneur, focused on results more than detail.
- Influence - Likes to be collaborative and involved, relationship focused.
- Steadiness - Calm, dependable doesn't like to be rushed, likes a supportive role and people person.
- Conscientious - A person who places emphasis on detail and quality, expertise and competency.

All these areas are treated as equal and we can have tendencies in more than one area, after all it is our life experiences and situations that have also shaped the way we behave. Understanding yourself is one of the first steps to self development. Understanding others makes you more tolerant and better equipped to understand how others priorities may differ from yours. This knowledge then impacts on how you deal with individuals, in a selling environment or even presenting a case to the board. For example if you are talking to D they want results not necessarily the ins and outs of how you are going to get there. If you are talking to C they will want specifications and analysis to be sure that they are making the right decision. This is a big subject but hopefully with this overview you are now starting to see how we gain a much better perspective in situations to both preventing or at least understand the quick emotional reactions that occur.

Also to help to understand our people & culture more there is another factor that we need to focus on - how do we make them feel? My mission is that everyone can love what they do and do what they love, part of this entails empowering and enabling them to pursue and fulfill their own personal vision. I started off by asking you to write about what you really wanted on your personal journey, and this has got to be aligned with everything you do. What is it you want to do with your life, are the actions that you are taking now congruent to that outcome or not? Why would you drive a change that didn't serve you in some way? A major factor in a process are the human links, what does the next individual need? Can you now see why understanding your people and their aspirations and personalities is so vital to analyse why a link in the chain / system may be broken? If your staff can relate to the change and are emotionally connected, they will be motivated to make it happen.

A great model that can help you start to understand some key issues that need to be addressed and fulfilled for your team to feel happy to engage is the SCARF model by David Rock. David summarises important discoveries in neuroscience about how people interact socially including how social threats and rewards can be received with the same intensity as physical threats and rewards. Studies at the time showed that the capacity to make decisions, problem solve and collaborate were greatly reduced under the threat response. If this is the case why is there still so much of the command culture within companies?

The SCARF model involves five domains of human social experience:

1. **Status** How you feel in terms of importance to others
2. **Certainty** How secure / stable the future looks
3. **Autonomy** How in control you feel over events
4. **Relatedness** How safe you feel with others (friend or foe)
5. **Fairness** How fairly and just you feel people are treated

David's theory says that if any one of these five are activated in a threat or reward situation they can activate the primary threat and primary reward reaction in the brain. For example, a perceived threat to one's status activates similar brain networks to a threat to one's life.

The model enables people to easily remember, recognise, and focus on maintaining the core social domains that drive human behaviour. If we are able to fulfil these criteria for our team to create a true sense of belonging and feeling valued then why wouldn't they give their best to help the company in succeeding in its mission? It creates the win win in the relationship that everyone needs; when you look at the company purpose being achieved in fact it becomes a win win win! In fact it gives us creative ways of motivating our team which are not all centred around monetary reward or power systems. Developing these long term relationships and cultures are far more sustainable in the long run.

People are our key asset; improving these relationships and social interaction factors is the secret to increasing engagement and productivity. Ultimately your success formula to buy-in for your vision and change.

Use the next page to take time to make notes about your current work climate; ask others how they see it even a supplier or customer you have a good relationship with that spends time on your site.

Exercise Time

Exercise 7 - What is your company climate like?

How is your leadership, do you lead by example? Do you understand the needs of your people? Take time to interview others.

"Knowing others is intelligence; knowing yourself is true wisdom. Mastering others is strength, mastering yourself is true power." **Lao Tzu**

Exercise Time

Exercise 8 - How do your team feel?

Ask yourself how you would rate the SCARF factors. How do you feel the team's needs are being met?

Exercise Time

Exercise 9 - Are there any developed 'norms' embedded?

Is there a strong sense of 'this is the way things are done around here'? Are there department barriers or a them and us that has evolved?

Exercise Time

Exercise 10 - What triggers problems?

Is there a particular situation that causes a lot of tension or friction within the company e.g. customer complaint? Think about the keys figures and their behaviour in these scenarios.

A final word on people

How you choose to turn up to work will reflect on others and they will echo your behaviour. if you choose to be totally present and focused on them they will engage; if you are distracted they will be disinterested.

That is why I asked the last question the way individuals react in a situation will have a knock on effect on everyone else. This reaction is often the effect on the climate that is being nurtured within the organisation.

We have now looked at how things are done in your company and you should be getting a feel for issues and concerns that have been voiced. This is a good step to acknowledging the way they feel and starting out on the journey to change things.

Things to observe over the next week:

- What mood are you and other leaders in when you arrive at work?
- How do individuals behave around you during that day, do they speak freely?
- When situations arise note key reactions and individuals.
- Assess your team strengths and weaknesses. How do members of your team react to another's weak or strong part of their character? If possible think about personality profiling or use books such as Tom Peters Strengthsfinder.
- Listen, Listen, Listen for the signs that dictate the way of life!

Observations from
the team and
culture assessment:

Hold on to these observations as they will be key to your approach, change strategy and tactics.

Next we are going to move back to looking at the systems and structure that support this climate.

Method & format of the system

So how is your system looking? Think back to exercise 3, 5 & 6, how did your systems evolve. System is a term that is widely used often in conjunction with management systems such as Quality, Health & Safety or the Environment. I quite often get asked if I am in IT when I mention systems; here I want you to just think of a system as the interaction of many processes to achieve a common goal. In this way you will be able to see that even if you do not have anything written down there will be a way of doing things or a procedure that people generally follow.

So why if you have a procedure does it fail or do you get complaints? Think back to who created your procedures; were they experienced individuals or new recruits? Did you take time to involve the people that were actually performing the tasks? Are individuals happy with the way things are done?

I want to teach you my steps to walking your business process, which we will get to later in this book. If your process is not working, you may have fluctuating costs, have trouble guaranteeing results or delivery, maybe things get missed or documents/ information are hard to find. If people are avoiding tasks and finding shortcuts don't play the blame game it is usually because there is something in the process that is not right. You need to find a way that fits with your team.

System stands for - Method, Order, and correct Sequencing. Whenever there is an unsystematic interaction, call it human intervention or preferences, your goal can only be achieved in a random manner. If people are doing things their way not the system how can things be consistent? If you do not get consistent service what do you do? Go elsewhere!

So thinking back to how we create procedures; when you give the task of sorting the chaos or writing your procedures to an inexperienced individual how can it be designed to your satisfaction and your vision?

A lot of us that have creative, innovative and entrepreneurial minds do not like to focus too much on the detail. If we do not want to give the attention and detail required for defining systems and processes, we either leave it or delegate. If you delegate you need to ensure that the right information is given to allow them to understand your vision, how well do they know you and the business? I am trusting that now you are starting to see the power of the system and how it maps out the customer journey backed up by your team. You need to take ownership of the design for the customer journey and vision that started off as your dream. The rewards will be worth the effort.

So what format can we use?

The answer is anything you like! Without wanting to go into much of the psychology on the way we learn, we all need to process information in a different way. The different styles of learning are usually visual, physical (learn-by-doing), or audible; with instructions we also need to break this down even further. Would your team prefer to use pictures, images, diagrams, colour coding or flow charts? The situation and environment we use the information in also affects what we need and how we process it. For example, in a quick response situation reading lots of text is much less appropriate to scanning the steps on a diagram/flow chart.

My tip as a start is that before you start, you need to at least assess the following:

- Where will you need the information to be (e.g. shop floor, out on visits)
- What style do your team like to see information - (e.g. visual, written)
- How will the information be used - (e.g. checklist, training only, scripts)
- Is it internally or externally visible - (e.g. seen by your public or customers)

I want you to understand what is appropriate to your business and team. In exercise 5 & 6 we briefly thought about what format your current procedures are in, a work instruction, a checklist or even a training video; nothing is wrong if it fits, people like it and it achieves the desired outcome.

What I want you to do here is, knowing the important factors to think about when creating your procedures / processes, what would you do in an ideal world.

Let's do some blue sky thinking for a moment then use that to give us a different perspective on our improvement plan later on.

Exercise Time

Exercise 11 - In an ideal world how would you create a new procedure in your company?

Currently if you were to introduce a new product or service how could you design and communicate the new procedure? How would you train people and prepare them for change?

Exercise Time

Exercise 12 - How would you know the new process is effective?

How would you know if the process was working, how would you assess and mitigate risk in the change?

How did you do? Was that a challenge? You should find it easier at this stage because we are starting from scratch and only looking at one particular product or service. Also this an ideal situation, no complications. This is just a single element of a system, but we need to document the whole business in detail or re-evaluate what we have. The problem is that when we look at the whole business we can experience such a feeling of overwhelm, and it seems such a big project, that we don't know where to start. Hopefully that is why you are reading my book, this is also what the exercises are about. I want to help you reason out and assess what you require and then plan a way forward.

So let's think about the important things to consider when assessing and writing the contents of a single procedure or process?

What level of detail do they need to do the job?

- How much relies from on the job training and professional judgement? Do they have enough guidance on boundaries for decision making in these cases?
- Who is the main owner of the process, who is in control?
- Is the technical content and level of details appropriate to the user?
- What resources do I need?
- Is it in a format that is easy to understand and relevant to the location where it will be used?

A final word for writing your system

Firstly, do you have enough information to write the process, are you involving the team? It is important that everyone that will be affected by the process gets to contribute. This can be done in stages of working groups and further consultation, but ensure all who matter feel they have been asked and they are valued.

Make sure you keep things simple, flow chart or list steps first. Plan the documentation or media that will be used and ask what your team would find helpful. Only create what is necessary, based on risk and control of outcome.

There is no right or wrong answer to what you need in terms of procedures, it is all about fit for purpose. Ask the team what would help them do the job more effectively and be able to train others.

Only create what you need to to control and mitigate risk and ensure a smooth running business. Keep it simple and logical.

Make sure you involve everyone that the process effects, they need to know their opinion is valued. Ensure that there is room to grow and allow innovation.

Things to observe next week

My challenge to you here for the next week is to take time out to think about what processes make up your business system and the input, output, and boundaries of the processes (refer back to the diagram at the start of this book).

- Think about what factors influence your ability to deliver, how do you control or make allowance for these.
- How do your team get the information they need and is there anything that would make their life easier.
- When is the workflow in equilibrium? What internal and external forces throw it out of equilibrium and disturb your peace?

Ask questions, observe and listen. Make sure that you fill in your light bulb moments and notes for action!!

The challenge in today's society is to design our business to be robust enough to manage change and be flexible enough to allow you to upscale and grow.

Control & reliability of the system

For a stable system we need to ensure we are planning, managing, improving, recording and controlling. How you organise these responsibilities will need to be defined. Sometimes the management element of a system can be misunderstood. Systems consist of a series of actions and decisions, the complex area is that of decision making. Human interactions involve different personalities and styles.

After discussing vision I normally ask my clients what are the day to day decisions that need to be made to deliver your vision. Decision making can end up being the black box that exists at the various stages of the process between inputs and outputs. Leading to a high dependency on individuals rather than the system. For this reason we need to look at boundaries and other factors that make up the components needed for a process to work; what guides your team when they have to make decisions?

The ideal situation is - to have actions that are specifically defined and to ensure that people are engaged with the vision. This way decisions can be made clearly in a way that correlates to the big picture you have designed. A simple example would be setting boundaries on financial spends, this enables people a clear boundary of when to escalate a decision. Making a judgement call on how to deal with a concerned customer or random situation is not always easily defined, this is where understanding the vision and values of the business backs up the decision making process.

My guidance is your story/ your purpose, this is what makes you stand out from the crowd. When your team understand what you stand for they will deal with the customer in that way.

When looking at your processes it is important to include the 'what ifs'! What if this doesn't happen who decides what to do, what is the new path? Who needs to be involved?

A recent example I have seen of this is attending a networking breakfast. The organiser forgot to book and the chef was not in early to cook the breakfasts also no staff to greet the attendees with coffee. The Meet started at 8am and the chef turned up for their regular shift at 8am to be met by a lot of hungry people. So what happened? The chef said she would get onto it straight away the breakfasts would go ahead and may be a few minutes later than normal but they would ensure we could all have the meeting. Shortly after a member of staff arrived who quickly got everyone sorted with drinks.

Now they could have said sorry you didn't book and it was too late to start preparing 20 breakfasts now, no we were a customer that needed help and they were going to go out of their way to make it happen for us. They understood the importance of service to the customer and everyone was suitably impressed.

This also reflects how the staff are treated if they are looked after and valued they are going to value the establishment and what it stands for.

Sitting above your processes and part of the control will also include the testing and auditing of your system, how do you prove that what you have set out in terms of your process works? Think about your performance criteria and KPI's (Key performance Indicators), once defined you need evidence and data to back this up. The data you collect on your system will then allow ongoing refinement but most importantly it will give you the feedback to make continuous improvement decisions and show you your system design is effective and supporting your business vision. Things will run more smoothly and give predictable results when you practice fact based decision making and get away from assumptions and fire fighting situations.

Over control

A quick word of caution on reacting to data collection especially figures - don't over correct or over control. For those familiar with statistical process control you will know what I mean. If you haven't come across it, the basic theory is this. There is natural variation in everything we do, trends go up and down. If we jump in and over react to changing trends we will add additional variation into the process. What we need to look at is the average outcome and any special circumstances where data goes outside of our expected range of variation. Quite often if we adjust before we need to we will get greater figures out of our range / tolerance limits because we have caused our average to move. If we had not adjusted we would stay around our nominal target with normal variation instead of manually causing a shift or drift from our aim.

So what do we need to control? What are either the critical decision points in your business that need defining or outputs that are critical to the process? Where are the biggest risks that need control, or maybe are currently causing complaints or have lost you a customer.

What do I mean by risk? The things that keep you or your staff awake at night, issues that worry you or cause dissatisfaction to your interested parties (e.g. customers, suppliers, neighbours, shareholders, legal team etc..) I would like you to spend a few minutes thinking about this for the next exercises. Be mindful that risk could be a wider threat or opportunity to the business if it has an impact on your ability to deliver your vision.

Exercise Time

Exercise 13 - Where do you monitor and control within your current process?

What is the critical path of your customer journey and the decisions that need to be made or specific critical outputs?

Exercise Time

Exercise 14 - How do you guide your team?

What current boundaries and guidelines are in place for decision makers?

Exercise Time

Exercise 15 - What measurements do you use for your processes?

How do you monitor your existing system and measure performance, KPIs (Key performance indicators or Critical success factors)?

A final word on effective control of your system

You should by now have an understanding of the purpose and values that drive your team's behaviour and ultimately affect decision making.

Through the last few exercises you will have started to identify key points in the process where you will need to focus on control. Also thinking about how you prove a process is effective and some KPIs that could be monitored to check on progress.

These things will be important and develop into the critical characteristics within your process as you start to look at mapping it out in detail. Remember it will be a balance between detail and competencies.

Things to observe over the next week:

For the following week I would like you to observe all the places you are recording information, ask people if they prepare reports for anyone. Then find out what the information is used for and who uses it, how much does it tell you? Is it actually used? You would be surprised at the number of times I find data being collected but going nowhere, maybe it is just too time consuming to collate but could be useful - is there a way it could be filtered or processed? Do not put up barriers think outside the box with technology much is possible so note everything down.

I want you to really think about the last exercises relating to critical steps, decisions, method and control. As we start to look at the critical path and decisions made we are in fact designing the skeleton of our processes and system. Remember we need to have a process to address all possible answers of a question ('what ifs?').

An interesting exercise is to carry out this thought pattern on critical decisions and control for one particular process then go and look at what is actually being done in practice by walking the process. You may find that what is needed v's what is actually done maybe two different things; it heavily depends on the approach taken when the business system was created.

When we start to design our system we are bound to try to follow logic and reason in our effort to discover linkages between inputs and outputs. The trouble is humans are not always logical and carry a lot of baggage. This is why it helps to have an independent person sometimes with a new perspective and not a history or attachment with the company or individuals. People become attached to 'the way things are done' and it's the emotional factor that prevents a true picture of how things need to be.

"After living with their dysfunctional behaviour for so many years (a sunk cost if ever there was one), people become invested in defending their dysfunctions rather than changing them" **Marshall Goldsmith**

What tends to happen in practice is that you have a great team trying to take the business to the next level but processes are being created in isolation. They may be created to solve a problem and that is great, you find a solution and systemise it. What is missing is the big picture view.

The main point I want to emphasise here is not to lose focus on the big picture when designing a process, consider the impacts it may have on other processes and the business direction. When you ensure that everyone understands your vision and the part they play, they should be pulling in the right direction, if they have access to the big picture and they know how they impact others around them they begin to understand the changes required.

I believe you have to satisfy two things here. Your company needs a focus and a purpose which needs to be in line with what you believe as an owner. You cannot be passionate going in a direction that is against your core beliefs.

Secondly you need to address the values and needs of your team, be sensitive to what they want out of life and enable them to flourish in the environment you create. If they are on a different path help them find it and let them go, you need this harmony.

Real change is about changing relationships both inside and outside the organisation, I can still remember the days when we would make a metal widget but not know where it went exactly. The relationship was mistrust, secretive not sharing and collaborative. In ISO9001 they added a phrase "mutually beneficial customer / supplier relationships" and that is exactly what we need. Win/win situations and a supportive supply chain, your system doesn't just rely on you, understanding the context of your organisation is key.

If you want dramatic change you must focus on process and relationships in harmony.

Looking at the following diagram you can see that if we want to be reactive and suddenly drive in a different direction, everyone needs to pull in the same direction. If we don't, we work against each other and the gears stop driving. The links in the chain of your system are the key to your success, not just the processes/procedures themselves. When the company is small imagine it like turning a tug boat it's not difficult just a small crew to communicate changes to. Now imagine the large company like a cruise ship; that turn becomes a lot more critical, timely and dependant on key functions and communications.

Applying this approach when defining your system will result in a clear definition of objectives for individuals. Linking them to the goals and direction of the company, it will keep everyone focused in the same direction. Suddenly turning that massive cruise ship seems more like a tugboat again because of the extra help, push and effort in the direction you want to go.

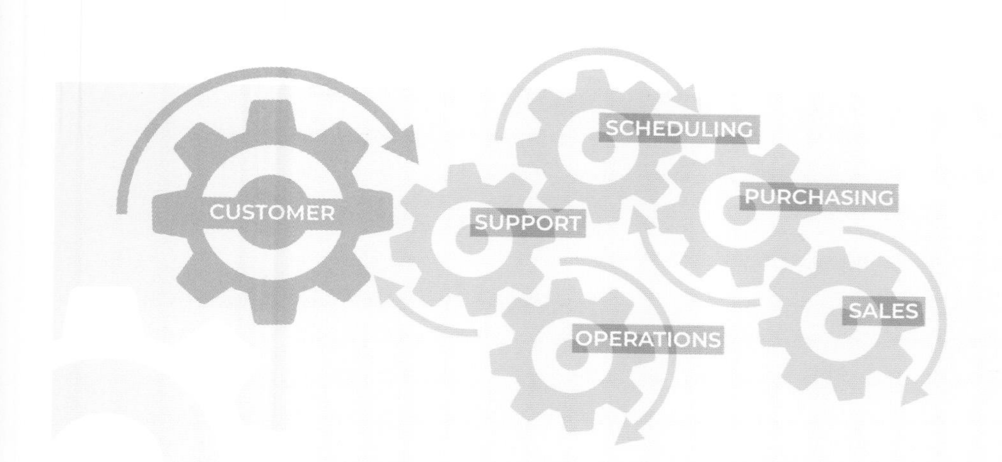

As you work through you must try to understand that for your people to adopt and agree to these objectives they must be part of the thought process. By using this level of engagement your managers will not only become systems oriented but start to recognise problems within the context of the company and its objective and naturally try to align with what they believe and support as the new common goal / vision that you paint.

When you get the right person in the role of coordinating the project people become open to collaborate across traditional departmental boundaries or even old fashion ivory towers that sometimes still exist (us and them). When you break down the barriers you can adopt true root cause analysis with cross functional teams and solve issues that have got deep rooted and stuck. Taking a systematic approach to problem solving is a whole other book but will reap rewards and give the most optimal solution and cost savings. People no longer focus on whose job it was or a blame culture they look to solve the system error together.

I think it's time to pause and absorb this information so I would like you to take on a little project over the next week, this needn't be just your opinion you can be creative, do a survey whatever it takes to find out a true perspective.

Things to observe over the next week:

Exercise 16 - At the start of the book we looked at how well your staff know your story and how they fit in, now's the time to go out and ask:-

1. How well do you think you share your company vision and story with your team, how involved have they felt?

2. Do you think your team from manager to front line understand the part they play in achieving the company vision?

3. Find out across all levels what the vision is in their eyes.

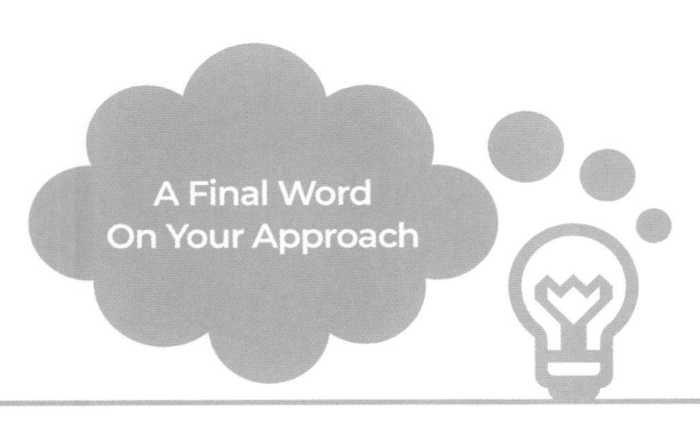

From taking time out to work on exercise 16 I hope you can see that sometimes there is difference in what we perceive to be the situation and the reality of what other people understand. Did you find any differences, how did that make you feel? How did people react to being questioned about the company?

You should now have a good awareness of the barriers that exist within your company and probably have a good idea of who your change champions could be.

Keep using those light bulb moments to record important thoughts and notes!

Let's look at the last topic - resources.

Resources

You do not need a big resource to make change.

In the last section we talked more about our team and how they fit in because they are one of your greatest resources. Resources can often be a sticking point and sometimes an excuse for not getting things done, or done fully. At times we may need to invest in our processes, but it is sometimes the smallest changes that can give the biggest results. For example changing your telephone answering scripts, this could have a dramatic impact on customer conversion. How much does changing conversation cost? Very little, but if you get a 10% increase on Sales? This may be a very simplistic example but there are many things that can be done before the need arises for big investment. The trick is to prioritise, and if you need to make small changes first to gain financial backup to invest then that's ok. Improvements to your business will only work when you take action, facing a big change can make you stop in your tracks so just make sure you evaluate, prioritise and just start!

I cannot emphasise enough to use your team, they have a wealth of knowledge and experience. You need a clear line of sight between your vision, objectives and the front line, they need to understand how they contribute to the big picture. By engaging people as early as possible they start to own the ideas and changes, change management becomes a whole different animal.

You could embrace suggestion schemes and tools such as Kaizen (refer to Appendix D). When you manage schemes like these correctly and keep momentum going, you will be amazed at the ideas that can be generated. The important thing is to keep communication going, manage people's expectations and always celebrate success. Some of the biggest failures I have seen of schemes like these are either they are pinned on monetary rewards and the whole debate of worth gets in the way; or there is just not enough resource put into managing the scheme and people are left wondering what happened to all the suggestions and brilliant ideas.

A word of caution: these schemes if rolled out company wide very quickly can produce large quantities of ideas that very quickly mount up. If people work hard and contribute and nothing gets done or feedback is missed, very soon they will not bother and things are much, much harder to launch a second time around. Be prepared.

Know your process, know your numbers and harvest the ideas of the whole team - you can produce the most amazing proactive culture together.

I would like you to think about the current issues right now in your business, try to list all the common problems which you see on a day to day basis. Try to stay focused on your business process rather than staff issues (although disgruntled staff tend to be a side effect of a poorly designed business process). This will be part of the observations for the next week, you can build on this over time and use it to spark discussions in your teams.

Things to observe over the next week:

Exercise 17 - What are the day to day issues that you see within your business?

1. Is there something that keeps cropping up, but the immediate solution seems too big at the moment ? Have you asked your team if they have any suggestions? Are there department barriers or a them and us that has evolved? Do you welcome changes and ideas from your team?

2. List anything here and think about how you got to know about it (grapevine, staff suggestions, complaint, observations etc..)

A final word on Resources

How did you get on, were there lots of little improvements that cropped up? Small changes can be used to create quick wins and help the change process get established. They are quicker to implement and drive motivation for more, people feel valued as their contributions are listened to. These findings and observations will be important later on as we look at our process, it will be interesting to see how many issues are related to gaps that may become obvious as you draw them out.

Resources like everything else need to be managed, you need to honest and communicate what the company is capable of doing right now and what will have to be planned into the future growth of the company. Share the journey with your team.

Chapter 3:

Learnings and journey check-in

The Personal Journey check in

Check in with yourself at this point, what are you feeling right now? You have delved into many aspects of your business, answered questions that you may not be used to. If problems came to light how are you reacting to the new information - are you taking things and holding them personally?

It is important not to go into overwhelm, you may be thinking why on earth have I made you look at so much stuff; what's the point? You will have to trust me and the process right now as you will each be going on your own journey and will have come across different sticking points and issues during this last chapter.

The idea and aim is just to absorb, take time to process what you have learnt on a personal level too before you proceed.

Recognise what may need to change but accept that some of this is your opinion and perspective, going into the mapping process with an open mind is essential. Everyone views a situation differently and will have their own way of solving a problem, you want to harness the power of the brilliant minds around you to find the best way forward together.

Notice in yourself your own reactions to different situations, people and information - why are you reacting in this way? Use each interaction as a personal healing point to identify your limiting beliefs, embedded emotional history and move through it.

There will be learnings on many levels throughout this journey and every conversation has a purpose, there is a reason you picked up my book!

What a lot of information to process in one chapter but an essential part of exploring what we understand about our current situation and what will affect the success of the project we are embarking on.

Let's summarise what we looked at:

PEOPLE

- We looked at the company culture and whether people's needs were being met.
- We thought about what triggers friction within the company.
- We thought about the profile of our team and the way we react to others.
- We learned how important the company story/purpose is to process and decision making, keeping all the gears pulling in the same direction.
- Involving everyone is key in improvement programs and managing expectation through the changes.
- We also assessed how much people understood on the part they played in the vision, including if they knew the vision for the future of the company.

PROCESS

- We looked at what format our process/system is in.
- We thought about how we would create a process and assess its effectiveness.
- We learned what is important to consider when you need to create a process.
- Keeping things simple and logical is the best policy. Only put in what you need to control the process.

- Starting to look at control we thought about decision making in out processes, where do we need control and evidence that it has been carried out?
- We looked at what is currently being recorded and measured in our business and whether that data is being used or not to make effective decisions.

Chapter 4:
How do we look at the big picture?

So in Chapter 2 we have been thinking about all the things that affect our business process, and current challenges that we face within our business.

Are you ready to make a difference? If so then read on because this is where I share my practical approach to process improvement. We will get right to the route causes together then plan and deliver the change you need.

I always recommend taking a snapshot of the business before you do anything, a holistic view to take in the big picture. By carrying out a complete process review you always have a reference point to refer to and with which to celebrate how much you have achieved. So what do I do? A process map with a difference! My method gives you a picture, and a picture that says a thousand words. There are many tools and variations out there to explore but you need to keep things easy to understand, that way everyone can understand the big picture and get the light bulb moment.

When you research your business in a systematic manner it is surprising how many changes that start to become very obvious that need to be made. Resist doing anything until after you have done the snapshot. Why? Because change needs to be planned, researched, tested and communicated.

The picture - The process map

So what does this picture or process map look like and how do you start? In this chapter we will go through how to conduct the review. I would like to start with basic steps to building and looking at a process map. If you have seen and understand flowcharts you will know how this works but let's refresh our memories.

Each step of business process is represented by a square and the flow between them arrows. When you reach a point where questions need to be asked or options addressed a diamond junction is used. Take a look at the following simple diagram.

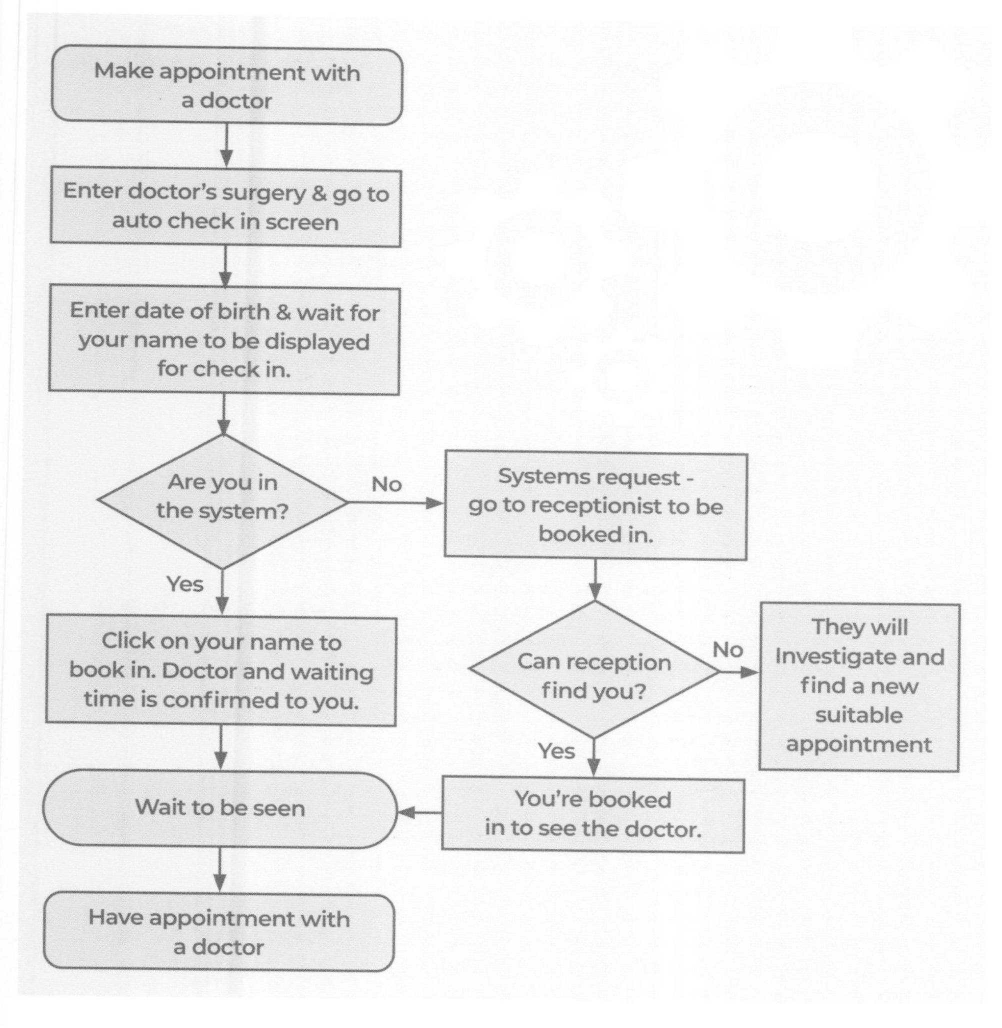

You will find a guide to some more common shapes and uses in Appendix C (note they are not the standard flowchart definitions). I want to use the simplest shapes for the most common issues I see, and if things don't fit invent your own! Who is to say what you use, the goal is a picture that everyone gets. If you are in the creative industry use your skills, maybe a storyboard theme. The key is to make sure you get the details and the important links in.

As well as the basic flow chart steps we will be adding data flow, who does what and where it goes. Email, production data, information sent out, received documents and management reports. This is the difference in the view I take on the system and the perspective I want you to learn & adopt.

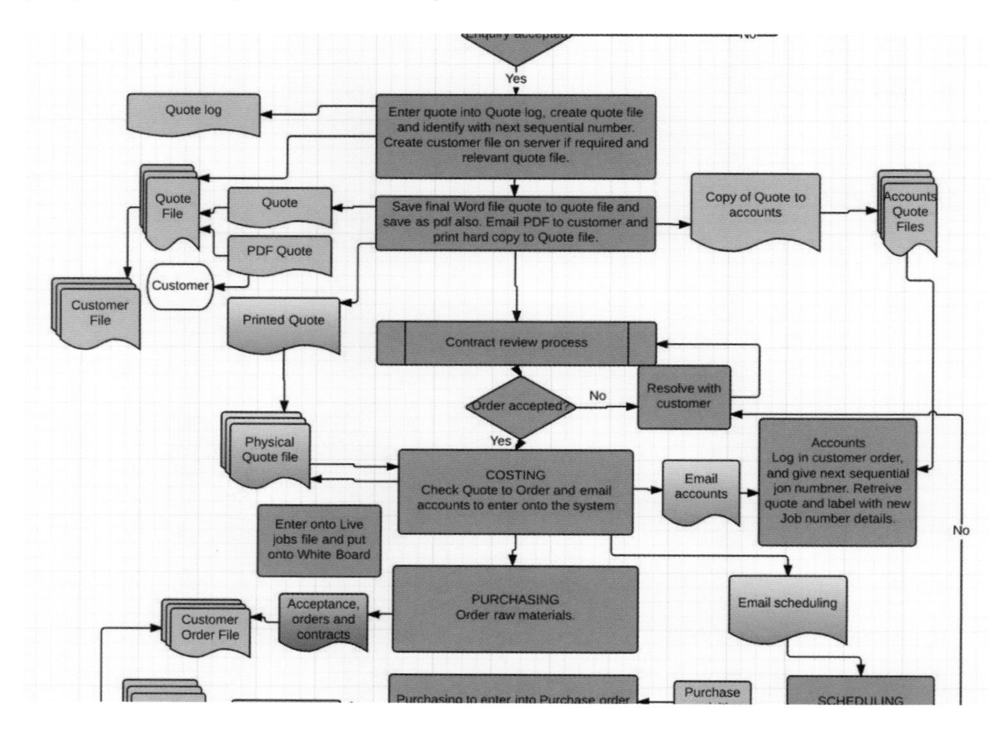

This is just an example of my style of process map. Can you spot areas that are crying out for automation or re-routing? Maybe where a company could invest in a common database (a project I quite often find myself managing to reduce risk and duplication).

Colour coding is very useful, if you colour code the type of role e.g. Admin, ops, financial you can see if it is a good fit for the person carry out these tasks.

What will you be looking for in your chart?

As you build up the process map you will be looking for duplicated tasks, documents, risks to the business and gaps where things are not controlled or consistent. I have listed some examples of what I commonly find but your gut instinct should kick in here. Of course an independent perspective can really help here so call on your team, mentors or outside inputs and perspectives where you need it.

Most importantly talk to everyone as you go, how do they feel about the way they work. If there are two different ways of doing things note them down, don't leave anything out. Look for:

- Duplication of data and documentation
- Duplication of roles
- Duplication of actions
- Non value adding actions
- Information journeys that are not streamline (too many involved in the decision)
- Lack of delegation
- Functions that overlap each other or run parallel without communication
- Areas where there are gaps, or maybe it's nobody's role / responsibility it just gets done by everyone.
- Manual data entry, e.g. multiple spreadsheets, word templates & pdf's, or Photoshop for instruction creation.
- Actions that are critical to the process but are not checked until the end or sometimes found by the customer.
- Data storage, many systems.
- Version control on documentation, multiple versions around at once.

My advice is when you create a document like this take time to absorb the picture, put it on the wall, encourage your team to add to it until you are satisfied that you have everything on it.

DO NOT DO THIS IN ISOLATION - It can be very easy to get carried away and fired up about sorting out the business, planning for the future, designing your perfect process. I want you to be able to grasp not just what people do but how they feel about it, building a close relationship with your team. We don't always know the best way of working and in larger companies when you revisit areas you may find yourself hearing the statement "we haven't done it that way for years now we ....". Wouldn't it be better to find out these things before you put all the hard work into the new process map?

So how do we go about finding all this out and creating a picture of how things work - the status quo? What is the best process to follow for drawing and mapping out our process?

Simple you WALK & TALK IT!

Walking the process - The initial review

When was the last time you walked your customer journey from start to finish and spoke to everyone on the way? How do they feel about what they do? What challenges do they face and what resources do they need? Remember here your people skills, don't use acronyms or ambiguous phrases and terminology. This is especially important if you are in a technical or financial industry, if they do not understand you the response will not be true. Be natural and talk their language, if you know your skills are lacking in this area or you don't feel comfortable get someone else to do it.

One person gave me some good advice as I was starting out on my networking journey; 'don't over think what you are there to do, just be friends and be friendly and watch what happens'.

I think this is very apt here just get a feel for what is happening on a day to day basis, remember this can be a delicate task. This is especially true when there are underlying company politics or culture issues to deal with, your team may want to air their opinion in a confidential way. In these situations I find myself often in a counselling / mentoring role, individuals are so grateful for the opportunity to unload their woes and talk to someone. This process of mentoring individuals has in itself the ability to facilitate change. Especially when they know that comments are kept anonymous and that they are being listened to and supported.

Another way to look at this is your own personality type and how well you can conduct this review, there may be things that you don't expect and at this stage you must not let emotion and defensiveness come into the picture - you are information gathering, do not take it personally.

My advice is to select your person to conduct the review on the following basis:

- Exceptional people skills
- Exceptional communication skills
- Tact and diplomacy, be sensitive to the feelings of others
- Someone that everyone will open up to, sometimes people fear talking to their boss due to risks of making waves or losing jobs.

- The person will need to hit the ground running and need to absorb a lot of information quickly.
- Good interpretation and analytical skills to translate information to process flow.
- Knowledge and understanding of flow charting / mapping is always a good start.
- Good patience
- They need to be open minded and without judgement or emotion about the issues being discussed.
- Treat information confidentially and be discreet.
- A good knowledge of the whole of the company operations.

Got the person in mind? Great, so how do you make sure that the review works?

The Review process

What exactly are you going to do? Walk the customer journey! All relationships internal and external are important but we are going to start with the most important - the customer experience you give. It is totally up to you how far you take the boundaries of this review but I like to reach out as far as possible - for example you may want to include areas like the following:-

- Start at the point where your customer is just an opportunity, a lead. How do you store those details, nurture that lead, what information gets sent out, from who how is it controlled? Who is responsible for making sure all of these tasks get done, how is it monitored? (There are many things that take place before you get an order)
- How do you process an order, review contracts, manage changes, acknowledge and thank customers. What formats or media do you use to communicate, how standardised and branded are your communications? Is it in customer language not technical jargon?
- How do you check specifications, authorise purchases, organise labour? Maybe you use external suppliers and labour, what information do they need to do the job right first time?
- How do you check and guarantee that things are being delivered in the right way?
- What actions spark the invoicing process off, do they have the right information when they need it? Are systems disconnected is there a more automated way of doing things?

These are only a tiny fraction of the questions you might address as you start to look more deeply at the way things are done.

So start at the beginning and ask yourself some simple questions at each step of the way, you are just asking people to share their experience and what they do so please remember this - just listen don't correct or give your view on how it should be done. We are looking for decisions and trigger points that enable things to move on from one stage to another; we are also looking for the must haves in the inputs that make the step successful.

Just ask "And then what" at every stage

Always ask "what if" or "what next" until you get to the end of the line.

Then ask "How do I know this is happening", evidence and control.

Then ask "What do I need to make this happen", resources & responsibility.

Then "Why do we need to do it this way" where applicable (you do not want to put people into defence mode). Maybe phrase it "do you think this is the best way of doing it" or "has this always been the case".

(Remember there may be many options or routes so record each one, you can't have too much detail at this stage.

"Success is the sum of details" **Harvey S. Firestone**

You need to take your time and be very thorough, another similar quote I like is this;

"Success is where preparation and opportunity meet" **Bobby Unser**

Which is exactly where you should find yourself with this exercise. You need to take enough detail to walk away and draw the flowchart for every part of the business and depict how they interrelate.

Some write a list of statements as they go, some fill out a table, some draw the flowchart as they go. There is no wrong or right way to carry out this exercise; you do what suits you. Just make sure it is logical there is lot of information to process and refer to when you sit down and write it up after the event - I know believe me. Set aside plenty of time for this exercise. You need to process the information quickly whilst it is all still fresh in your mind do not leave it for weeks before creating the flowchart.

Here are some guidelines and rules to help you before you start and to make you think about the types of questions and recording method you want to use.

Guidance on walking your process

- Write down the Goal/vision for your process / customer experience.
- Note what triggers the start of the process (there may be more than one).
- Write down 'WHAT ACTUALLY HAPPENS NEXT'
- If different people approach tasks differently make a note of this.
- Make a note of responsibilities, who are the individuals carrying out the tasks at each stage.
- Work in steps or stages of the process, so that you can clearly note the inputs and outputs for each.
- Think about the conditions that have to be in place for each step to be successful, what if they don't happen make sure you map out alternative routes.
- Make a note of what resources are used, people software, systems, forms etc..
- What triggers the end of the process, critical success factors.
- Take your time, you can revisit go back and ask questions, the important thing is to get the basic flow right.

Make sure you write down any light bulb moments as you do the review, things that work and things that don't work as you talk to your staff.

Exercise Time

Exercise 18 - Gather your data.

Walk your process and gather all the information to draw up the process map. In the next chapter we will be looking at how to draw up the final map.

Record light bulb moments here.

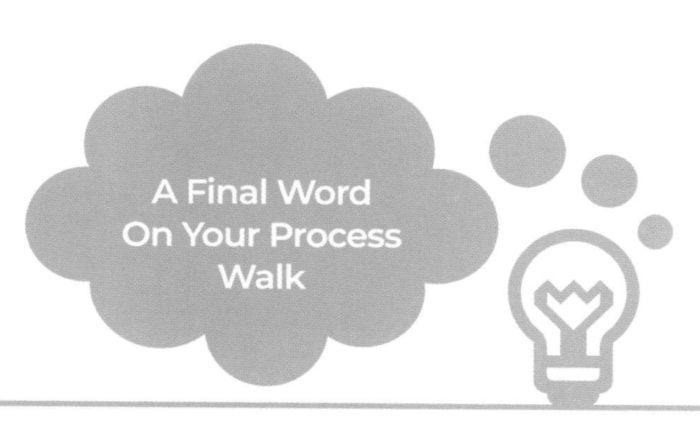

You should by now be happy with the look and feel of the process flow approach and what you need to look for in your own snapshot process map.

We have talked through the process of walking the customer journey and included everyone in gathering information, not an isolation exercise for you to write up the process. You may have decided that you were not the best fit for the exercise and delegated it based on the criteria listed for the profile required.

How did you find it? Did you get sufficient detail? If not don't be hard on yourself keep going, ask more questions and take time to gather the data. Remember you can pin it on the wall and get team input involve others in the journey.

In the next Chapter I want to help you gather your thoughts on what you have found so far, so before we proceed observe what has happened as a result of this exercise.

Things to observe over the next week:

How has the exercise of process mapping had an impact on day to day behaviours and actions?

1. How well do you think you did? Has it impacted positively or negatively on relationships around you?

2. Do you notice anyone starting to bring ideas to the table or wanting to change and become involved? (take note of these ambassadors/champions for your change process)

3. Just observe and then refer back to your initial observations in the earlier exercises; make a note of any differences.

Chapter 5:

Gathering your thoughts and mapping the process

Try and picture each part of your process as a series of steps and each one needs to be defined. I want you to imagine the process as a series of customer-supplier relationships in a chain.

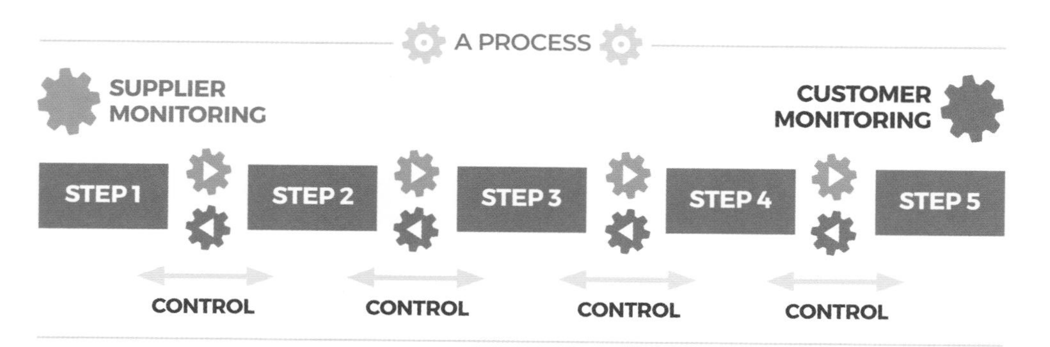

When we set the right boundaries, expectations and requirements at each stage we will have happy customers throughout the company. This is what I call creating harmony in the workplace. Taking things step by step will enable you to understand the most complex of processes, and with your map you will be able to keep the big picture in mind. As you make observations record them, have a post it wall for ideas (an ideas car park to prevent shiny object syndrome). You can organise this stage in the best way to suit your team, ready to hold a brainstorm. You need to share the process map, gather ideas, sort and prioritise so again putting it on the wall will help. You will use the information that comes to light to plan improvement and automation, how and when these actions take place I think comes down to prioritising based on two things:

- **What is going to have the biggest impact on the business in line with your strategy.**
- **What is the financial impact; what is currently within your resources that can be acted on now.**

You need to drive engagement and enthusiasm, you need big wins without too much impact on your resources stretch. You do not want to put your team under stress at the start of your amazing journey. It all comes down to careful change management - the need to prioritise and plan wisely.

It will be amazing and you will be **surprised** and **delighted,** which are sometimes words that seem alien when talking about your business system. I want to ensure that change is embraced to make your journey easy, if you draw the chart in the right way change will be self-evident to a lot of people. Most will be grateful that you are going to help them resolve the niggling issues of everyday, getting smaller successes in at the beginning can be a game changer. People may not believe that changes will actually happen, especially if you have promised and not delivered before; for example projects that have been started, momentum lost and efforts faded. Experiences like failed improvement projects can have a huge impact on the next time you try and achieve something together.

"Everyone has accepted by now that change is unavoidable. But that still implies that change is like death and taxes - it should be postponed as long as possible and no change would be vastly preferable. But in a period of upheaval, such as the one we are living in, change is the norm," **Peter Drucker - Management challenges for the 21st century.**

Take time to understand your team as they could be going on the journey with you but the other voice in their head may be the negative one preventing them from believing it will work. If this is the case it will also hinder their true creativity for innovative ideas to move forward, the quick wins help gain momentum and build a positive experience with the change program. The more positive experiences they have associated with your plan the more they will get on board and be ready to change. It is a bit like buying a new car, they want you to attend the grand unveiling and the test drives and trials. Every positive experience leads to a better result at the buying decision. Mindset work here would be extremely beneficial because if we can develop our people to have confidence in their potential and fire their desire to learn we can foster growth.

As you progress, praising hard work and effort will help to cultivate this growth mindset and willingness to work for the good of themselves and the company vision. Mentoring individuals may be the answer for some so explore all individuals, what drives them and motivates them? Taking time out as you walk the journey to understand their aspirations and how they feel is another key part of this journey. When I carry out this exercise with my clients I am able to report back all issues and culture and it is like I have been there for years. I know them because I have taken time to know their people as well as process.

Think how you would feel if you make all the effort to gather this process information and then do nothing productive with it; you have to take big action to make it work. Don't set yourself up to fail because you put all the effort into the exercise and not to the after support. Be aware of your own needs through the exercise, don't let overwhelm creep in. It is easy to get overwhelmed by too much information coming in or ideas; and when we are overwhelmed we are not in a productive state. If you feel yourself becoming overwhelmed due to pressures of work, personal life and this intense exercise then STOP - Pause take a breather get clarity on what you have done so far before gathering any more information. When we get stuck in this way in any situation of our life it can be easier to take no action because we don't know where to start, there may even be a new path and vision to follow which can be daunting. These are common occurrences I see in people during these stages of growth, especially if your outlook for the future has changed in what you want. Creating a picture of your business can make things much easier to understand.

The process map then becomes a catalyst for instigating the desire for change within your team.

Exercise Time

Exercise 19 - Draw your process map

1. Draw your flow chart, be creative, make it easy to understand.

2. Make a list of improvement ideas as they come to light.

The Personal Journey check in

Are you suffering from a little stress or overwhelm at the moment? How do you stop yourself going into the doldrums and affecting your health? Here are some tips to keep you working through the project

Overwhelm

STOP / PAUSE / BREATHE – Yes I know it's the last thing you want to do right now. The wheels mustn't stop turning, got to keep everything moving along. You need to connect with your breath and yourself, check in on you and what's going on, learn to create that calmness and mindfulness for a moment.

If you are worried about something ask yourself "Is it mine?" Are you fretting over something to which you have no control? If yes then let it go it is not your journey, if you cannot change an outcome by your actions then it is ill focused action. Focus where you can make a difference.

When we just have too much to get done and no time there are various options. You can put more hours in but this is a short term / emergency option and probably the route to overwhelm and exhaustion. The biggest one we tend to ignore is to ask for help, put a brave face on. Another person may not always be able to give time or take a load off but you will get another perspective and friendly support. If you have a team effective delegation is key and this can be an issue for some to let go of responsibility to others. Paying another individual or company is always an option, but what if the only option you see is just you?

We sometimes need to learn to accept that we can only do what we can do, if we have got ourselves into this position the question is why, so that we can focus on taking steps to ensure we do not let it happen again. The problem is when you are in this state it is not easy to get clarity and plan solutions. We therefore need to lift ourselves up with a mixture of quick wins and feel good prioritised actions.

Quick wins (easy actions to close out quickly) could be a way of helping you also but cannot take away the larger stuff that is looming over you. Therefore I believe you need to tackle some of each. Choose a couple of things that you can complete easily and quickly; when you start to tick things off your list you will be motivated to carry on because of the feeling it gives you to strike them off the list.

Next ask yourself what one task will make a real difference to the situation and make me feel great if I complete it? Again feel into it and get emotionally attached to the vision of you successfully reaching your goal.

Now focus on this one thing and one thing only and keep at it until it's done, no distractions. When your done make sure you celebrate, feel good about your achievement. Then pause, breathe and repeat.

You can vocalise what you are focusing on to another, then you have an added accountability reason to pursue the action. I practiced all of this today and shared my goal with someone I met networking, told them to ask me next time we spoke. I have now had the most focused session on my book instead of dipping in and out of things that need to be done.

One thing to add is that a to do list is isn't time bound we may have an expectation of when it will be completed, like a weekly task list. Usually there is no information of how long each item will take us, so how do we expect to know if the list is achievable by the end of the week? Lists like this set us up to fail at our own targets and cause overwhelm, I teach my clients a simple planning process that removes lists and uses other methods to qualify tasks and write action plans that work, are achievable and simply get things done so you may need to work on your planning if you still use lists rather than plans and default diaries.

Motivation

Sometimes we find it hard to stay motivated when things are taking longer than we first thought, this is why I ask you to connect emotionally with you end vision and share with everyone. The more emotionally connected we are the more driven the action, it is not about the system but what this process will deliver. There are many benefits of going on this journey and I hope that you are starting to see the difference in your team and relations already. At any time you can stop and revisit exercises if you feel you have not got the desired result, use your learnings and get the team together to focus your actions. Sometimes after a failure we can stay positive and be more determined to put things right having a fighting spirit, other times it can leave us deflated. Usually after a few wobbly moments we are in danger of depleting our resilience to these things. During this time it is key to find some tools that help us overcome any loss of drive and energy we experience, try these

Look after you

Make sure that you have not changed any of your good routines such as your health, exercise, meditation, affirmations, gratitude or journalling and leisure time. If the project has encroached on your focus and personal time then you need to recharge. We have all heard the saying fit your own oxygen mask first, you need to be in a good place for your business to be in a good place. There is more to this because taking away any of our needs just as we considered the SCARF model in exercise 8 when you affect basic needs your relationship breaks down with the project and so does your connection and motivation.

Share with others, use your support network

We all know people that just seem to raise our energy and are armed with positive quotes. Use your support network to keep you going when times get tough, in fact you can arm yourself with inspirational messages, quotes and reading. Reading other stories can fill you with inspiration and daily reading is so good for us. Sharing your mission and having others who believe in what you are doing willing you to succeed can make all the difference trust me it is part of my journey.

Visit the alternative, what happens if you do nothing?

Make sure you visit the pointers about why you started on this journey and recognise the impact of doing nothing and returning to the way things were. Stopping might bring a reprise or reduce the workload but you lose the reward that you are working so hard for. You are not alone on this journey many have had to systemise find others and share experiences, what did they do? If you get stuck and cannot answer a question I am happy to be messaged just join in the discussion in the Facebook group around this book - BUSINESS JOURNEY FOR TIGERS.

Are you celebrating your wins?

The beauty of journaling your journey with this workbook is that you get to revisit the steps, recognise what you have done and the thought process needed. Are you taking time to celebrate what you have done so far? Make sure you not only plan out your steps but include the way you will celebrate achieving these steps with your team. In fact a bigger question what will you do when it is finished? We all need something to look forward to so plan the big reveal and launch of the new you, project completion it can excite the whole team.

Visualisation

We haven't spoken too much about one of my favourite subjects when mentoring, vision. When we go to the movies in our mind it can be very powerful, if you truly connect emotionally the energy and vibration you put out is truly infectious. Try it with anything you desire in life and work visit your vision for 5 mins every morning (no long meditation needed), then act as though you are already at that point in your life. Because you are feeding the universe constantly with the right energy and you live in a state of true belief you will be returned with the right opportunities to make it happen.

Do not search for these opportunities. You will know when they appear and are the right thing to do, you will feel it in your gut. The best way I can describe this is if you had your heart set on buying a specific design and colour car you will start to see it everywhere yes? Had you not intended to buy that car you would probably not have noticed them, they would just be another car passing you by. Reality rises to what the mind devises!

> Give your visions and thoughts substance through assigning feelings and emotions.
>
> This will allow the energy and vibrations of your vision out into the universe and
>
> attract the right energy back to you. I believe this is how thoughts become things.
>
> **A. Fumpson**

Chapter 6:

So what now, using your process flow mapping to drive change?

A client recently said to me about their newly mapped process "I love it but I'm not sure what to do with it, put it up on the wall?" This is a phrase that I am hearing a lot of at the moment, "thank you so much for the process map, but what next?" It is good to have a passion for where you are taking your business this map has to be a catalyst in creating the next phase - the change process. The problem I have recognised is that a complete map can give you so much detail that you can't see which step to do first.

Prioritisation & Planning

From your process maps you will have areas that need to change and new systems that could be significantly different to what people are used to. As more and more view the process flow more ideas will get added to the ideas car park! The Ishikawa or fishbone diagram in Appendix B can also be a good idea here to brainstorm solutions for each improvement, you need to gain a consensus of opinion for each idea put forward for improvement. There will be easy quick wins that are simple to do and your champions for change could be set on tasks to get the program started, the remainder of improvements need to be organised and planned.

These changes need to be carefully prioritised being conscious of the time and resources needed. You are not going to get the support and engagement from your team if you start putting them under too much stress, and likewise for yourself when you take on too much. Take careful note of the current pain points and issues that you looked at under the people and culture section, be mindful of the things that people told you on your process walk. All of this should arm you with knowledge on how to plan the journey.

Itemise the areas in your process where you have found risks, gaps, duplication of tasks, inefficiency or possible automation. You can always add to this list as you find other things on your process map. This list can be split up into areas to help with project planning, for example the Sales Process, Finance and accounting, Operations or handling customer concerns and improvements.

I use my own tool (see example in Appendix D), It will enable you to think about the individual improvements and their impact on the business. The list of actions get rated or scored on impact, resources, investment and timescale, the result is a prioritised list based on fact. It can help explain the assessment process between two improvement ideas, especially when you have a conflict of opinion.

Don't set yourself up to fail! Plan changes step by step have a detailed program of events and resources, remember to include the quick wins to boost morale. It's all about the strategy, the team and how you celebrate the wins and share the journey together.

Make sure you have the time and resources available BEFORE you execute your plan; there is nothing worse than having a team fired up and innovation stifled because they cannot access what they need to succeed.

You can also take your map to the next level and rewrite a streamlined version, draw up what you think it could look like then you have something visual to work towards. Having a clear picture of what you are aiming for will help the team to make decisions in line with the end picture.

We discussed the approach earlier in the book so here are my tips for approaching the next step to process improvement.

We will also look at the relevant points from your exercises to be mindful of when preparing to change.

Create the buzz - Be prepared to share, listen and refine

Share your vision/utopia, get people excited about what you are trying to do, put your new streamlined map on the wall! Involve your team in discussions, ask their opinion. This may sound obvious but there are many businesses I talk to where it is not their first thought to involve team right down to the front line.

In the early chapters of this book we looked at what people were using for information and explored the top 3 reasons for you doing this exercise will as well as the top three benefits for your team. Use this knowledge, build on what you know works well. Take those reasons for doing this exercise and add the opinion of others where appropriate to build momentum. Create leaders at every level willing to share the vision and reason for change. When you are transparent and honest in what you do, listen to others opinion and explain why; you will get a much more favourable response.

Look at the framework

Make sure you revisit your values and vision together, are they complementary? Is everything you want to do in tune with your core beliefs and purpose? I often say that one of most important questions after 'what is your why?' is 'what are the the day to day decisions that have to be made to achieve your goal?' if you want your team to make great decisions they must first have to understand your direction & purpose.

In chapter 2 you looked at how well you shared your story behind the business - if this is not clear make it so before proceeding. Share to newer staff where you started out as well as where you are going.

Be mindful of any conflicting views as you revisit the interview information from walking the process in chapter 3. Is the culture supportive of your values and new direction?

Communicate the program for change

Once you are crystal clear on your objectives and project plan they need to be communicated. I don't mean a poster on the wall, live and breathe them, lead by example and get your team on board.

If you believe in your program with a passion, and tell your story to others, then your team around you will start to live and recall that story. Make sure all of this is communicated to the outside world too if appropriate. It may benefit your customers and your sales - for example new technology or extra capacity.

Not many people like change, even less when they don't know what is going to happen. Fear will set in and they will make up a story where there is none. We need to cut cost, jobs will be lost, the company's in trouble; you know the drill we have all heard this type of gossip. Don't let this happen to you, nurture open communication.

Shout about the big plan, the game changer! You want people to be excited about the end result and be part of it. Emotionalise it, what is your story behind the changes; why are the changes needed? It is ok to be vulnerable. People would rather hear you, not the mask we sometimes wear to cover issues. You can choose champions for the projects and channels for the feedback such as notice boards, internal communications or social media. You need a platform that can be used to celebrate the success stories and the challenges ahead. If you are open about the choices you make, even if you make wrong decisions, being honest will gain you support. Not everything will run perfectly, you are human after all; what defines us is how we rise after a fall. Learn from everything and turn it into an opportunity for improvement!

Take action

Now for the essential bit, once you have a strategy for change you need to start taking action. If you are redesigning part of your process ensure you consider the big picture and links on the process map. Be mindful of the impact your changes can have on other areas of the process, the company goal and customer experience. Always follow the discipline of root cause analysis, prove your chosen solution, test and install. The success of your plan is down to you taking responsibility and action - if it is something you are excited about it should be infectious!

Listening & Feedback

It is really important that you listen to all concerns and questions and make sure you feedback progress. There is a big danger that people get carried away and assume that everyone has the same level of knowledge. There will be many pockets of the company especially in larger organisations that will be champions in their own right keeping business as usual going on. That doesn't mean that they do not want to hear the latest news and story or be involved in the celebrations, it is a team effort keep everyone in the loop.

Celebrate achievements & milestones

A very important thing - celebration. Change isn't an easy path so don't forget to stop and give yourself a pat on the back and everyone involved. For you personally as I have already stated, I suggest that when you do your business planning that you write down the reward you are going to give yourself and your team for each milestone and do it!. Have fun and celebrate in style.

Also, if you are doing great things talk about them, quite often there is work going on with the community and charity that don't ever get mentioned, (I was guilty of this in the beginning).

Keeping everyone motivated

You cannot make others be 'motivated' you can only motivate yourself and hope that it is infectious. Action comes from ourselves and a desire to participate. Sure you can get people excited and fired up but it is that long term motivation you are after to sustain the changes. Motivation comes from truth and a truth within us - when people realise the truth about what they can become or achieve it changes their lives. They have to believe it and they can only believe in you if you are honest and open with them, the authentic you.

What your people need is a clear understanding and strategy for viewing their potential and mapping out goals and the part they play in the journey. It has to be in line with their own values and goals, be worthwhile to them, believable and achievable. Use the tools I shared earlier under Motivation in Chapter 5 and share them with your team.

Embed the change, support the transition

When you make changes do not overwhelm and change to much at the same time. Make sure people are comfortable with things before you move on. Your leadership, support and understanding at this stage will be critical to the success of the project. If you want a fun exercise to demonstrate what happens in change and where and why support is needed then check out resources on www.white-tiger.co.uk it will help others understand what is happening within the struggle for change.

A final word on change

Systems is not all about logic and sequence it is about people working together in harmony to achieve a goal. People are not always logical and then there is this thing called culture too. Do not underestimate the major impact these have on change, put the work in to gain a deeper understanding before you start. When putting people and process together in this way, communication and knowledge is key, I encourage you to think about your company as a learning organisation, become dynamic and fluid. Be flexible and don't restrict yourself by what others believe. I know with the right direction, guidance and support you will always get where you need to be. Trust in your own vision and heart, take others on the journey with you - those that don't were never meant to be on that journey with you.

> "It is not the strongest of the species that survives, nor the most intelligent, but the one most responsive to change." Charles Darwin
>
> "You are today where your thoughts have brought you. You will be tomorrow where your thoughts take you"
>
> **Ralph Waldo Emerson**

Vision, strategy, planning, testing, action, celebration

Chapter 7:

Lets recap

Lets recap! This chapter should help act as a checklist to what you have been doing so far. If you are unsure on any then stop, revisit and get more detail until you feel comfortable and confident to tick all of the boxes.

You have the status quo, you have seen where changes can be made, you have assessed the impacts of these changes and you have your strategy to take action right? Let's just check!

You know your status quo

- You know where your current procedures and practices came from
- You know what is currently in use around the company, paper or otherwise
- You have walked your customer journey
- You have listened well to your team on how and why they do what they do
- You have drawn your process map
- You have shared your map and got feedback

You know your company climate

- You have assessed the barriers within the company, e.g. department or them & us.
- You understand how things get done & reactions to situations (e.g. fire-fighting)
- You have looked at the leadership within your company
- You understand the profile of your team members
- You know the aspirations of your team, what drives them personally as well as in work
- You have looked at how much your team understand the company story and how they fit in - engagement

Angela has supported my business for several years, and as a thought partner has helped me shift my focus to work that reflects my passions and enabled me to make money doing what I love.

Tim Martin - Selling Service

You have thought through your approach to change

- You know how processes & procedures are created and changed at the moment
- You have assessed the main issues that affect you on a day to day basis
- You have assessed your process map and re-drawn where necessary
- You have shared your new process & vision
- You have made note of the pain points and issues that currently act as triggers and know what to avoid or pay particular attention to for your change program

You have planned the changes

- You have categorised the main improvement points found in the process map & feedback
- You have prioritised the improvements
- You have assessed your resources and scheduled to allow the improvements to go ahead
- You have assigned responsibilities and communication channels
- You have planned how you will celebrate
- You are ready to support the change
- You have shared your plan

You are ready to take action!

To achieve greatness: "Start where you are, Use what you have, Do what you can".
Arthur Ashe

Conclusion

You have the power to change - you don't need fancy titles and buzzwords just the right approach and people skills. I am not teaching rocket science this is my way of doing things - what I do know is that it gets results and it's worth sharing. Re-light that passion and excitement and share it with your team.

- Just remember take ownership of your business process and improvement strategy, encourage others to follow suit by honesty, integrity & open communication.
- Make it a compelling force - your energy is infectious.
- It must motivate, be clear on the why, what will it do for your team and their way of life.
- Whatever you do encourage education and training, become a learning organisation.
- Most of all have fun and celebrate.

Your system will give you the ability to deliver what you promise consistently, with predictable costs taking the guesswork out of running the business. Keep refining and improving so that you can spend less time in the job and more time on delivering that WOW factor that makes you who you are.

"Our goals can only be reached through a vehicle of a plan, in which we must fervently believe, and upon which we must vigorously act. There is no other route to success."

Stephen A. Brennan

Angela has been an invaluable part of my own on-going personal development. Angela brings a wealth of knowledge and experience in combination with a very personable approach allowing for free flowing conversation. Angela has provided me with support and counsel throughout a significant period of change management within the workplace and has played a key role in helping me to continue to develop as a leader for the future. My gratitude extends beyond words of thanks and more to the recommendation and encouragement to others to work with Angela to take the steps to further your own development.

Tristan Holloway - Yeo Valley Family Farm

Appendix A

ISO9001

What is it?

As Quality became a major focus guidelines were written to standardise the requirements for companies and ISO9001 is an international standard which forms part of the ISO9000 group of standards. ISO9001 is a specific requirement for a Quality Management system and you can become externally certified to the standard to demonstrate your commitment and ability to meet the requirements.

What are the benefits?

ISO9001 provides a disciplined approach to defining your Quality Management and especially how your operations will run.

Defining and meeting your customer & stakeholder expectations.

Consistency in the way your operations are run

Provides a good set of common practices to follow

Establishes good leadership in the approach

Doesn't allow you to stand still, you have to take action to continually improve.

Encourages fact based decision making

Certification to the standard gives a certain level of assurance to the community around you of your ability to meet requirements.

The reason for mentioning ISO9001 is that it is a good example of a structured method of following a system. It gives you a method to understand the needs of your interested parties, define risks and opportunities and with planning achieve consistent results. You are also required to work on continually improving your performance completing the loop.

A well designed Quality Management System will give clarity, create structure and control in the way things are run. I believe that the ISO9001 standard is a stepping stone to bringing the confidence back of customers when they look at organisations who have sought to gain and retain this certification. It is also built on excellent principles which should be adopted with or without the formal path of being audited. If you want a structured way to move forward and there are reasons that certification could be advantageous to your business commercially then external certification could be a path worth exploring.

Check out my blogs and website for more articles and support when making your decision on this one.

www.white-tiger.co.uk/blog

Appendix B

The Fishbone Diagram or Ishikawa

What is it?

The diagram is a cause and effect diagram that is constructed in a brainstorming type of exercise, it was devised by professor Kaoru Ishikawa in the 1960s. Ishikawa was a Japanese professor who made some key developments within the field of quality management, one of his best known was the development of the concept of the fishbone diagram, which is also known as the "Ishikawa diagram". He believed that quality improvement is a continuous process, and it can always be taken one step further spreading the concept of customer service to continuing after a product was received.

The purpose is to solve problems in a structured manner and so the arms leading off from the diagram are often categories to help with the problem solving process and root cause analysis. The typical categories are:

Man
Method
Machine
Materials
Measurement
Environment

At the end of the diagram (fishbone) is placed the problem statement that is being brainstormed for root cause. The shorter lines going into each of the main categories listed above are for the causes. Try to brainstorm at least a few possible causes in each category if you can, remember some causes can be mentioned in more than one category. Just be clear of the categories that you are going to use before you start.

Ishikawa also expanded Deming's four steps of Plan Do Check Act that we know so well when tackling issues, he splits them into the following six points which I believe are much more in engaging.

Determine goals and targets.
Determine methods of reaching goals.
Engage in education and training.
Implement work.
Check the effects of implementation.
Take appropriate action.

The Diagram

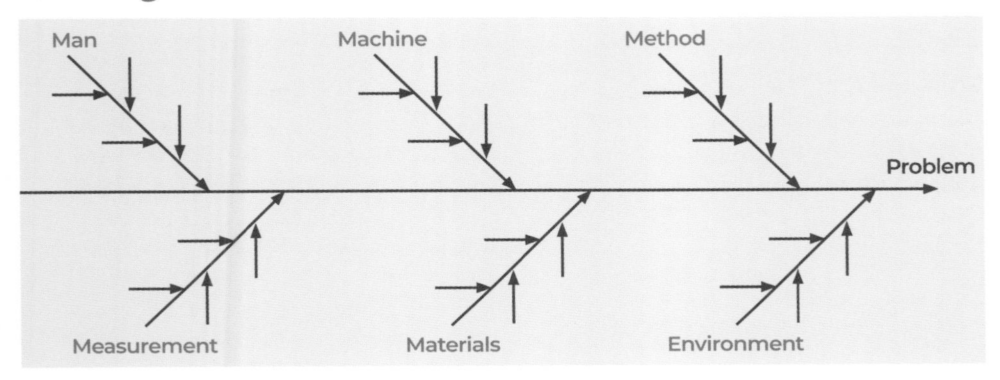

At the end of each arrow you would enter a possible cause for the problem placing it in the relevant category. For example if deliveries on time were a major issue then you might find a diagram building like this:

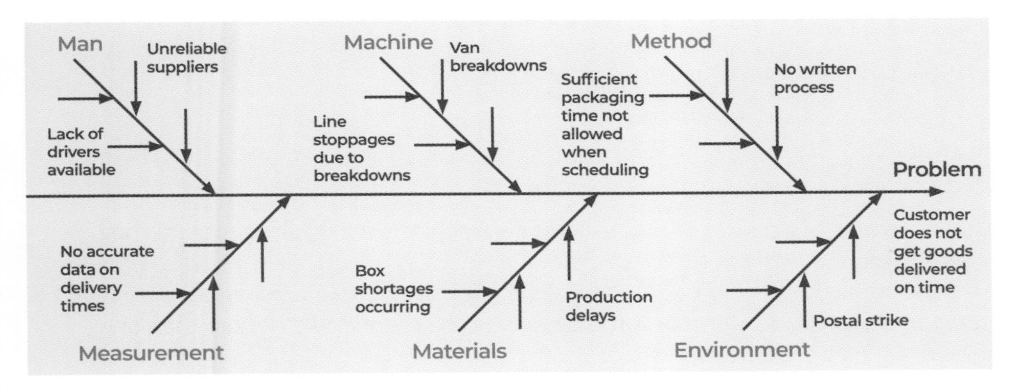

What are the benefits?

These diagrams can be used to facilitate your brainstorming sessions so that you maintain focus. It is very structured so don't let it limit the thought, however seeing all the ideas in one place clustered in this way can actually stimulate further trains of thought.

The diagram can be a really useful tool to then display to others what has been achieved and is flexible to leave up and add to if needed. People will be able to see the relationships between the ideas, any overlapping ideas and spark up further solutions.

Appendix C

Flowchart symbol ideas

What are they?

These are the symbols that are most commonly used plus a few that I like to use and my meaning for them. Remember colour coding through a chart can also be really useful.

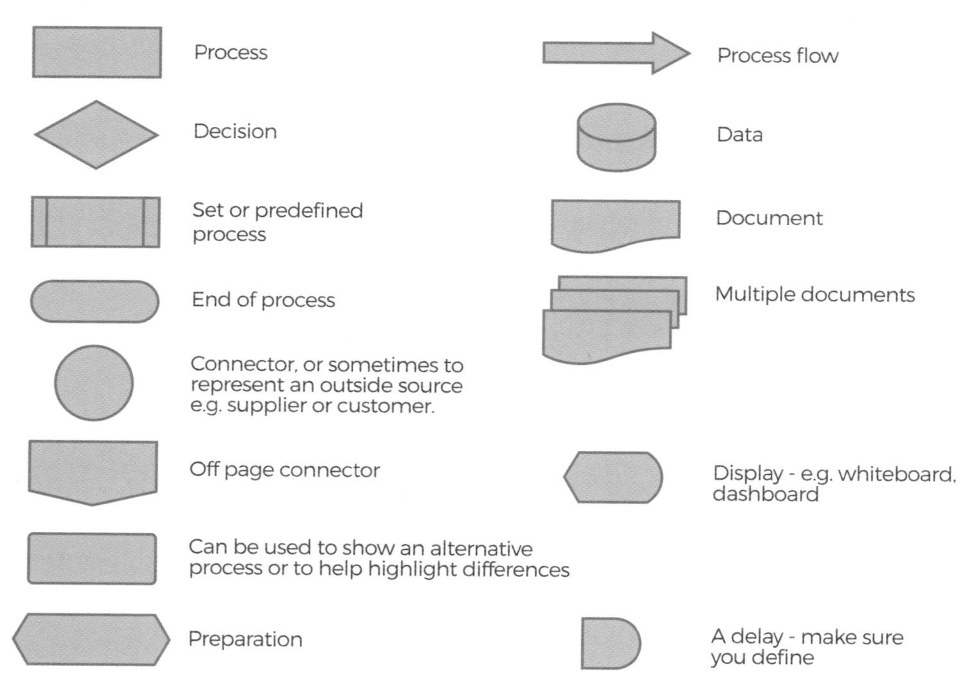

What are the benefits?

I think the benefits of using well known symbols helps others to understand what you are trying to achieve; however when mapping out for your team it is about a community developing together. Like I said earlier I have seen many creative businesses achieve great things and business plans that have been really beautiful works of art.

It is about creating something that people will resonate with, that maybe fits in with your industry. The more input others have in the creation the more they will engage in the process.

Appendix D

How to prioritise

Tiger Style!

This style table is based on a tool called PFMEA which stands for Process Failure Mode & Effects Analysis which although initially developed by the military is now a widely based tool for analysing risk and failure.

However I like to use numbers to demonstrate and quantify why decisions are chosen. As with this example it is surprising when you look at the risk reduction against the various solutions how clear options can stand out as the correct path. This table is in its infancy as I created it solely to aid my clients clarity but look forward to feedback on others using it.

PRIORITISATION TIGER STYLE TABLE 1

	Process improvement analysis										IMPACT						New figures			
Process description	Current system status	Current problem	Effects of problem	Sev	Occ	Current control	Det Risk	RPN	Solutions / Actions	Resp. & Date	I	R	T	S	CIN	Priority	Sev	Occ	Det	RPN
Answering the phones	Nil	Non-standard message going out to customers	Customer complaint	6	3	Nothing	8	144	Telephone script	JB End May 17	1	2	2	3	12		6	1	8	48
									Call monitoring	TS Jul 17	5	5	5	3	375		6	1	5	30
Booking and diarising appointments	Informal	Apponyments missed or double booked	Unhappy people	10	4	Nothing	8	320	Redefine single booking system / procedure	AF Apr 17	3	2	3	3	54		10	2	6	120
									Automated booking system	BG Jul 2017	4	2	4	4	128		10	1	2	20

The Table explained

Don't be put off by the look of it, some I know just wouldn't attempt it but after running through an example actually found it enlightening. I will keep looking at ways of making it more appealing to the eyes! Also you could think outside the box and add your own categories and weighting.

Step 1 - Enter the problem area and process involved along with the effects this is having. The current system status just means what is in place currently. We then have two ratings to give this:-

SEV = Severity, Rate out of 10 how much of a problem it is. (10 most serious)

OCC = Occurrence, Rate out of 10 how likely to occur the problem is. (10 most frequent)

PRIORITISATION TIGER STYLE TABLE 2

	Process improvement analysis			
Process **OFFICE**	Current status	Potential effects of failure	Sev	Occ
Answering the phones	Nil	No standard format for customer	5	2

Step 2 - Next you have to think about the Controls you have in place to prevent the problem, how likely is it that it will be picked up?

Det Risk = Detection Risk. We rate this ability to Detect that things have gone wrong out of 10. (10 means it goes undetected and causes customer issues)

Lastly is our calculation RPN = Risk priority Number this rates the issue as a whole and equates to:

Sev x Occ x Det = RPN

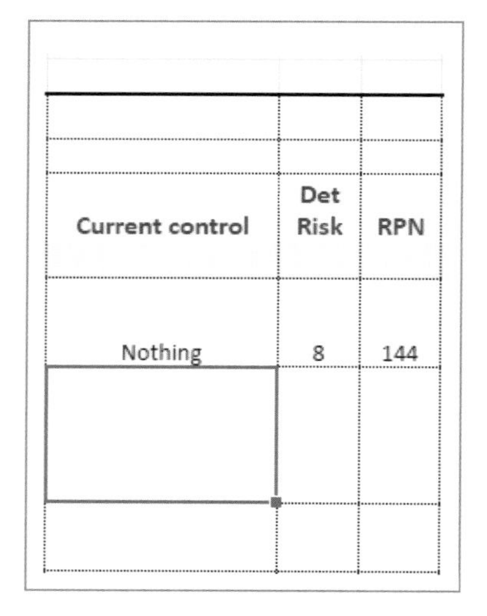

Current control	**Det Risk**	**RPN**
Nothing	8	144

PRIORITISATION TIGER STYLE TABLE 3

Step 3 - We now need to look at the proposed solutions that we have as there may be more than one. As below we enter the actions and rate them as follows:

I = Impact. Out of 10 rate the impact that this will have of the company financially.

R = Resources. Out of 10 rate the drain that it will have on resources.

T = Training. Out of 10 rate the extra training that will be needed.

S = Skills & Knowledge. Rate out of 10 whether you currently have the knowledge to do this.

PRIORITISATION TIGER STYLE TABLE 4

Solutions / Actions	Resp. & Date	IMPACT				
		I	R	T	S	CIN
Telephone script	JB End May 17	1	2	2	3	12
Call monitoring	TS Jul 17	5	5	5	3	375

The calculation is CIN = Company impact number.

CIN = I x R x T x S

Step 4 - Lastly we need to assess the new figures for the process after the proposed solutions have been implemented. There are figures that will not change like the severity of the problem however the likelihood of it happening and being detected could change as my example shows.

You carry out the same calculation for the RPN and see what effect your different solutions can have. Take for example our issue with dealing with incoming calls. A call monitoring system would be expensive to run compared to writing and implementing a script but there is no dramatic difference between the RPN results they give, but the CIN number tells a different story. In this situation you would most likely opt for a scripted procedure then put in further controls should problems continue.

TigerTime is a campaign of the David Shepherd Wildlife Foundation; an adaptable and flexible, non-bureaucratic organisation responding promptly to conservation threats by supporting trusted, reputable individuals and organisations operating in the field. Lean on administration but generous on funding, DSWF supports a range of innovative, vital and far-reaching projects throughout Africa and Asia, achieving real results for wildlife survival.